Microprocessor Systems

Microprocessor Systems
Interfacing and Applications

ROBERT J. BIBBERO, P.E.

Honeywell Inc.
Process Management Systems Division

DAVID M. STERN

Drexelbrook Engineering Co.

A WILEY-INTERSCIENCE PUBLICATION

JOHN WILEY AND SONS
New York · Chichester · Brisbane · Toronto · Singapore

Library of Congress Cataloging in Publication Data:

Bibbero, Robert J.
  Microprocessor systems.

"A Wiley-Interscience publication."
  Includes index.
  1. Microprocessors. 2. Data transmission
systems. I. Stern, David M. II. Title.
TK7895.M5B48   621.3819'535   82-1950
ISBN 0-471-05306-6   AACR2

For Becky and Josh, Barb, Herb, and Ira,
who will create and use tomorrow's microcomputers

Preface

Two trends in modern electronic systems are coming closer together —microprocessors and communication. Microprocessors are linked by communication networks, and the networks themselves are controlled by microprocessors. Within microprocessor boards and chips, components and functions such as memory, central processing unit, timers, and peripheral control chips are connected by data, address, and control buses. These are parallel communication links in miniature.

In spite of these similarities integration of distributed data processing elements (*nodes* in communication jargon) has come hard. With conflicting claims of Ethernet, IEEE Standard, S-100 bus, and the like, most microprocessor-driven products remain incompatible if they have different makers. Partly, this is due to the lack of industry standards and the rapid growth of the field. More basically, communication and computing systems have widely different origins and goals that are only now beginning to merge.

The primary communication facility in most countries is the telephone system—designed and optimized to meet the requirements of analog voice transmission and the ear of the receiver. On the other hand, data processing is mostly digital and tuned to the needs of binary electronic circuits. Digital data transmission and handling depend on the ultrareliable integrity of millions or billions of two-level signal bits. Now the voice telephone system and similar serial wire links are being used to transmit these bits, and what makes good hearing often causes slow and inaccurate binary signaling.

The intent of this book is to explain both the microprocessor and the data link in terms of signal paths and communication functions, and to show how they are made compatible. The modern digital computer, in fact, stands on three powerful concepts: binary representation, stored programs, and addressing. Two of these are clearly digital data communication functions, while programming is equally so, since it is the means by which users communicate with the digital processor. In this book we are concerned with all three of these concepts, and show how they can be used to understand and create powerful and useful systems.

The impetus for this new work has been the broad acceptance of the earlier book by Mr. Bibbero, *Microprocessors in Instruments and Control*, published by Wiley-Interscience in 1977. This book is targeted to the same audience of engineers, students, technicians, and managers who use microprocessors and design them into new devices and systems. In this companion volume we expand the coverage of microprocessor application principles and the hardware and software tools needed to implement them. It is intended to cover newer, more advanced, and broader topics than the earlier work.

For example, new applications of ever-increasing complexity have become feasible owing to the increased addressing capability of microprocessors, and the freer use of lower-cost memory has suggested emphasis on high-level language programming, rather than the use of assembly language. Two chapters have been devoted to high-level languages, including BASIC, Pascal, and FORTH as microprocessor languages. Likewise, the importance of digital data links for multiple microprocessor systems in factories and offices has dictated a chapter devoted to data highways, and the use of communication principles throughout.

Although *Microprocessors in Instruments and Control* was not specifically intended as a textbook, it has apparently filled a gap and has been well received as such in both colleges and technical institutes and has been used as a text for short courses and seminars such as those given by the ISA and IEEE. This new volume may be usefully employed in the second half of a two-period undergraduate course in microprocessor applications, and is recommended for such use. In addition, we have retained the self-contained self-study nature of the earlier work.

Robert J. Bibbero
David M. Stern

Merion Station, Pennsylvania
January 1982

Acknowledgments

We are grateful to many people at Drexelbrook Engineering Co., Honeywell Inc., and elsewhere for the encouragement and support that made this book possible. In particular we wish to thank Mr. G. V. Novotny, our Wiley-Interscience Editor, for his three years of patience, and Dick Webster and Renzo Dallimonti of Honeywell, Fort Washington, for their continued support. Mary Ann DiFalco performed willingly and with skill the bulk of the word-processing input (that which was not accomplished with the senior author's SYM-1, SWP-1 software, and MX-80 printer). We thank Ethel Trefsger for artistically producing the many graphics, and Janet Casey for coordination and secretarial help. A number of engineers at Honeywell, Drexelbrook, and other companies offered helpful support and criticism; among these we especially mention Yoel Keiles, Shams Huda (Pascal), and Ira Bibbero (FORTH). Of course, the authors retain full responsibility for all statements of opinion and any errors or omissions. Permission to reproduce microprocessor and other integrated circuit technical data, granted by Synertek, Inc., Motorola Semiconductor Division, Texas Instruments, Inc., Signetics, and Mostek, among others, is gratefully acknowledged

RJB
DMS

Contents

Microprocessor Systems

1

Addressing and
Digital Fundamentals

The dramatic decline in the cost of integrated circuit modules has led to their use in an ever-widening range of products. Removing the economic necessity to spread the cost of digital processing over many tasks has increased the range of applications even more by simplifying product system design and reducing the time and cost of product development.

The increased range of integrated circuit applications has correspondingly increased the number of people directly affected by digital circuit and microprocessor technology. This book aims to help any person familiar with relay and analog electronic circuits to make use of digital electronic circuits as well. The availability of integrated circuits as inexpensive modules allows their interconnection to perform complex functions without requiring a deep understanding of the circuits in the individual modules. The net effect of this revolution is to allow the persons working with them to concentrate their efforts on the system function, thus permitting a shorter time interval between specification of an idea and its implementation.

Only a small number of important concepts are involved in digital circuit system design. With these concepts in hand the designer can see the essential similarities between the components provided by different manufacturers, and will be able to select them on the basis of cost and specific features of interest.

The term *interfacing* refers to the interconnection of circuit modules. The considerations that apply to connecting integrated circuits on a circuit board are generally the same as those that apply to interconnecting system functions (or circuit boards), which are more widely separated.

ELECTRICAL ANALOGIES

The entire focus of modern digital circuits is electrical. Electricity provides the energy and the signal into and out of the circuit. This situation differs from earlier practice, where electricity provided the energy but the function of the device was an output in some other domain. For motors the output is rotary motion, for a light bulb the output is light, for a buzzer the output is a sound. For these applications of electricity the output of the device is an entity that can be immediately used by human beings. In the case of electronic circuits the output (and usually the input) signal is an electrical signal that is an analogue of some parameter, an analogue that ultimately must be interfaced to some conversion device which will render it useful to human beings. Included among conversion devices are printers, cathode ray tubes (CRTs, television screens), punches, and motors.

There are two forms of electronic signal representation. In what has come to be called *analog* (sometimes linear) circuits the analogue exists as a voltage or current whose magnitude represents the information being processed. The hi-fi amplifier is this type of circuit. In this case the information being processed is sound, the electrical signal is an analogue of the sound, and the ultimate conversion device is the speaker which renders the electrical signal audible to humans. The second form of signal representation is the *binary* number. In this case the electrical signal (or signals) has (have) only two states, referred to as HIGH and LOW, ON and OFF, or ONE and ZERO. The binary number requires multiple channels to make up a number, just as multiple columns are required to make up a general decimal number. That is, three columns of digits are required to form the decimal number 304. In binary notation this same number is written 100110000; it is seen that here nine columns are needed to form the equivalent number. Each column represents a place for a binary digit, abbreviated *bit*. In the decimal numbering system each column is weighted (multiplied) by a factor of 10 over the preceding column to the right. In the normal or *natural* binary numbering system each column is weighted by only a factor of 2 over the preceding column to the right, so it can be understood that many more columns are needed to form a binary number as compared to a decimal number.

BINARY NUMBERS

Figure 1-1 shows the conversion between normal binary numbers and the decimal numbers ranging from 0 to 16. Note that other binary

		(2^4)	(2^3)	(2^2)	(2^1)	(2^0)	
		16	8	4	2	1	Column weight (2^N)
		4	3	2	1	0	Column number (N)
Decimal numbers:	0	0	0	0	0	0	
	1	0	0	0	0	1	
	2	0	0	0	1	0	
	3	0	0	0	1	1	
	4	0	0	1	0	0	
	5	0	0	1	0	1	
	6	0	0	1	1	0	
	7	0	0	1	1	1	
	8	0	1	0	0	0	
	9	0	1	0	0	1	
	10	0	1	0	1	0	
	11	0	1	0	1	1	
	12	0	1	1	0	0	
	13	0	1	1	0	1	
	14	0	1	1	1	0	
	15	0	1	1	1	1	
	16	1	0	0	0	0	

Figure 1-1   Decimal to binary system conversion table.

numbering systems are possible, such as the reflected binary or Gray code, BCD (binary coded decimal), and so forth. We only consider the normal binary code at this point, however.

In Figure 1-1 the dotted lines are used to aid the perception that every time an additional binary column is added the digits in the less significant columns recycle in a regular manner.

To assemble a binary number, we use the concept of positional notation, just as we do in decimal numbers. For example, the meaning of the decimal integer number 7980 is actually

$$7 \cdot 1000 + 9 \cdot 100 + 8 \cdot 10 + 0$$

or

$$7 \cdot 10^3 + 9 \cdot 10^2 + 8 \cdot 10^1 + 0 \cdot 10^0$$

As the position of each digit moves to the left of the *least significant digit* (LSD), its value is multiplied by a weight that is an increasing power of 10, where 10 is called the *base* or *radix*.

Similarly, a binary number is assembled from powers of the base 2. Thus the binary number equivalent to decimal 304, which we noted, is

$$100110000_2$$

This literally means (in decimal notation)

$$1 \cdot 2^8 + 0 \cdot 2^7 + 0 \cdot 2^6 + 1 \cdot 2^5 + 1 \cdot 2^4 +$$
$$0 \cdot 2^3 + 0 \cdot 2^2 + 0 \cdot 2^1 + 0 \cdot 2^0$$

or

$$1 \cdot 256 + 0 \cdot 128 + 0 \cdot 64 + 1 \cdot 32 +$$
$$1 \cdot 16 + 0 \cdot 8 + 0 \cdot 4 + 0 \cdot 2 + 0 \cdot 1 \qquad = 304_{10}$$

(Note that we have used the subscripts 10 and 2 to represent the decimal and binary bases).

As a rule, to assemble a binary number, start with the largest power of 2 that is equal to or less than the decimal equivalent and put a 1 in the most significant place or column. This is 256 in the case of 304_{10} and the column or power of 2 is 8. Continue down toward the least significant digit, adding a 1 for each column whose weight, when added to the sum so far, does not cause the total to exceed the original decimal equivalent. If the weight of the column makes the sum too large, put 0 in its place and go to the next column. In the example 256 + 128 exceeds 304, thus the first two digits were 10 . . . 256 + 64 = 320, thus 100 . . . , but 256 + 32 = 288 < 304, thus 1001 . . . , and so on.

A simpler but less obvious way to convert from decimal to binary is to divide by 2, placing the remainder (1 or 0) in the *least* significant place. Continue to divide the decimal integer quotient by 2 until the last 1 is reached, which will be the most significant digit. For example, to convert the decimal number 26_{10} to binary, perform the following operations, then reverse the order of digits:

$$\frac{26}{2} = 13 + 0 \text{ remainder:} \quad 0$$

$$\frac{13}{2} = 6 + 1: \qquad\qquad 1$$

$$\frac{6}{2} = 3 + 0: \qquad\qquad 0$$

$$\frac{3}{2} = 1 + 1: \qquad\qquad 1$$

$$\frac{1}{0} = 0 + 1: \qquad\qquad 1$$

or $26_{10} = 11010_2$.

We have already seen how to convert in the opposite direction, binary to decimal, in our explanation of the meaning of binary notation (see above). Thus to go from binary 11011 to decimal we multiply each 1 by its positional power of 2 and add them:

$$16 + 8 + 0 + 2 + 1 = 27_{10}$$

HEXADECIMAL SYSTEM

It is worthwhile to spend a good deal of effort in learning how to handle binary numbers and arithmetic because a microprocessor operates only with 1's and 0's, representing the two possible states of its digital elements. However, binary notation is very lengthy and inefficient, and it is very easy to make mistakes. Most microprocessor programming is done in a more convenient notation called *hexadecimal*, which uses a base of 16. Since 4 binary digits can represent 16 different numbers (0 to 15 or 1111_2), each hexadecimal digit is equivalent to four binary bits. This results in a more compact and efficient notation. The hexadecimal system may be thought of as a shorthand for binary. Since the microprocessor continues to operate in binary fashion regardless of whether the user thinks in decimal, hexadecimal, or any other base, this is a very good way to consider the hexadecimal system.

The problem with using a hexadecimal number system is that we have 16 digits and there are only 10 Arabic numerals in our decimal base. Therefore we have to invent 6 more, which we will name (not very imaginatively) after the first 6 letters of the alphabet. Thus the hexadecimal numbers and their decimal and binary equivalents are

Decimal	Hexadecimal	Binary
0	0	0000
1	1	0001
2	2	0010
3	3	0011
4	4	0100
5	5	0101
6	6	0110
7	7	0111
8	8	1000
9	9	1001
10	A	1010
11	B	1011

Decimal	Hexadecimal	Binary
12	C	1100
13	D	1101
14	E	1110
15	F	1111
16	10	10000
256	100	100000000
4096	1000	1000000000000

Hexadecimal numbers use the same positional notation as that of any other base, except that now each successive significant column represents an increasing power of 16; that is,

$$16^0 = 1$$
$$16^1 = 16$$
$$16^2 = 256$$
$$16^3 = 4096$$
$$16^4 = 65536$$
and so forth

The hexadecimal number 1E7 therefore means

$$1 \, E \, 7 = 1 \times 16^2 + 14 \times 16^1 + 7 \times 16^0 =$$
$$256 + 224 + 7 = 487_{10}$$

To convert in the other direction, decimal to hexadecimal, we use the same trick as in binary conversion. Divide successively by 16 and put the remainder in increasing order of significant digits. Thus, to convert 6897_{10} to hexadecimal, perform the operations

$$\frac{6897}{16} = 431 + 1: \quad 1$$

$$\frac{431}{16} = 26 + 15: \quad F$$

$$\frac{26}{16} = 1 + 10: \quad A$$

$$\frac{1}{16} = 0 + 1: \quad 1$$

then reverse the order of the results:

$$6897_{10} = 1AF1_{16}$$

OCTAL SYSTEM

The *octal* system is used in some digital work, but not as frequently as the hexadecimal system. The octal base is 8, and the decimal numbers 0 to 7 are equivalent to 3 binary digits instead of 4.

Decimal	Octal	Binary
0	0	000
1	1	001
2	2	010
3	3	011
4	4	100
5	5	101
6	6	110
7	7	111
8	10	1000

The reader should, as an exercise, work out the methods of conversion toward decimal from octal using the principles described.

OTHER CONVERSIONS

To convert from binary to hexadecimal and the reverse is very simple, which is fortunate, as this is the operation most often used by the microprocessor programmer. Merely group the binary numbers in groups of four, starting with the least significant digit or bit (LSB), and convert each group to the hexadecimal equivalent. Take, for example, 305_{10}, which in binary is

$$0001 \ 0011 \ 0001$$

From the hexadecimal table we can see that these three binary groups convert to

$$1 \quad 3 \quad 1$$

hence the equivalent hexadecimal number is 131_{16}.

Converting in the other direction, hexadecimal to binary, is just as simple. Write the hexadecimal number and, under each digit, the equivalent group of binary digits (from the table). Take $3FE7_{16}$, for example:

	3	F	E	7
Binary:	0011	1111	1110	0111

Memorizing the binary equivalent of numbers up to 15 (four digits) will enable you to do these conversions quickly.

Converting from octal to binary and the reverse is done in the same way except that groups of three are used. (Remember in all cases to start with the least significant bit for the grouping, whether in 4- or 3-bit groups.)

Converting from hexadecimal to octal or vice versa is done by first converting to binary and then completing the transformation to the desired code by regrouping. For example,

$$B56_{16}$$

1011	0101	1100	binary

or

101	101	011	100	(regrouping)
5	5	3	4	$= 5534_8$

Hexadecimal multiplication is not often required in programming microprocessors, but could cause some difficulty. Although special calculators are available for hexadecimal and octal calculations, they are not always available to nonprofessional programmers. One solution is to perform the calculations in decimal and convert to hexadecimal. Multiplication can be performed directly using the usual decimal rules of multiplication, but it must be recalled that the carry refers to multiples of 16, not 10. The hexadecimal times table shown below is helpful in carrying out this operation.

01	02	03	04	05	06	07	08	09	0A	0B	0C	0D	0E	0F
02	04	06	08	0A	0C	0E	10	12	14	16	18	1A	1C	1E
03	06	09	0C	0F	12	15	18	1B	1E	21	24	27	2A	2D
04	08	0C	10	14	18	1C	20	24	28	2C	30	34	38	3C
05	0A	0F	14	19	1E	23	28	2D	32	37	3C	41	46	4B
06	0C	12	18	1E	24	2A	30	36	3C	42	48	4E	54	5A
07	0E	15	1C	23	2A	31	38	3F	46	4D	54	5B	62	69
08	10	18	20	28	30	38	40	48	50	58	60	68	70	78
09	12	1B	24	2D	36	3F	48	51	5A	63	6C	75	7E	87
0A	14	1E	28	32	3C	46	50	5A	64	6E	78	82	8C	96
0B	16	21	2C	37	42	4D	58	63	6E	79	84	8F	9A	A5
0C	18	24	30	3C	48	54	60	6C	78	84	90	9C	A8	B4
0D	1A	27	34	41	4E	5B	68	75	82	8F	9C	A9	B6	C3
0E	1C	2A	38	46	54	62	70	7E	8C	9A	A8	B6	C4	D2
0F	1E	2D	3C	4B	5A	69	78	87	96	A5	B4	C3	D2	E1

BINARY CODED DECIMAL

Since the hexadecimal, octal, and binary systems of numbers are not familiar to most people, most instruments, calculators, and other devices that have a human interface display or print their results in decimal notation. It is convenient to have a binary method of representing the numbers 0 to 9 which is standardized so that decimal information can be interchanged between devices. We do this by merely using the first 10 combinations of the 16 that are possible with 4 bits; this is called *binary coded decimal* (BCD) notation:

Decimal	BCD
0	0000
1	0001
2	0010
3	0011
4	0100
5	0101
6	0110
7	0111
8	1000
9	1001

The other binary 4-bit combinations (1010 to 1111) are ignored in BCD. Thus a 4-bit combination (sometimes called a *nybble*) can directly represent a decimal number if the device producing or receiving it "knows" that it is working with the BCD system. Some microprocessors have special instructions that enable them to interpret and produce BCD numbers and also to do BCD arithmetic. Most microprocessors work with 8 bits at a time (the 8-bit combination is called a *byte*; the nybble is logically a small byte); one byte can hold two BCD numbers.

BINARY FRACTIONS

Although the internal representation of a bit in any digital device is always an integer (whole number), either 1 or 0, it is necessary in programming to consider binary fractions. The fractional representation must, of course, be "known" or interpreted by the computer, just as the processor must be able to distinguish between binary and BCD notation.

The integer positional notation that we introduced identifies each bit as a positive power of 2, increasing as we go to the left of the LSB. In fractional notation we insert a dot, called the *binary point*, which is exactly analogous to a decimal point in ordinary notations. Just as numbers to the right of a decimal point represent increasing *negative* powers of 10:

$$0.123_{10} = 1 \times 10^{-1} + 2 \times 10^{-2} + 3 \times 10^{-3}$$
$$= \frac{1}{10} + \frac{2}{100} + \frac{3}{1000}$$

so do bits to the right of the binary point represent negative powers of 2:

$$0.1101_2 = 1 \times 2^{-1} + 1 \times 2^{-2} + 0 \times 2^{-3} + 1 \times 10^{-4}$$
$$= \frac{1}{2} + \frac{1}{4} + \frac{0}{8} + \frac{1}{16} \quad (= \frac{13}{16})$$
$$= 0.5 - 0.25 + 0.0625$$
$$= 0.8125_{10}$$

To convert a decimal fraction to binary we can use an approximate method. Multiply the decimal number by 2, use the resulting integer, and multiply the remainder by 2. The conversion of the decimal fraction 0.5921, carried out to four places, is

0.5921	0.1842	0.3684	0.7368
×2	×2	×2	×2
1.1842	0.3684	0.7368	1.4736
1	0	0	1

or

$$0.5921_{10} = 0.1001 \ldots {}_2$$

Unfortunately there is considerable error in this procedure, as we can see by converting back to decimal:

$$0.1001_2 = \frac{1}{2} + \frac{0}{4} + \frac{0}{8} + \frac{1}{16} = 0.5625_{10}$$
$$(0.5921 - 0.5625) = 0.0296, \text{ about 5\% error}$$

This error is the result of the neglected remainder 0.4736, which was not used. The error can also be calculated by multiplying this remainder by the last computed term, $\frac{1}{16}$ in this case,

$$0.4736 \times \frac{1}{16} = 0.0296$$

Because of the difference in efficiency of the binary and decimal bases, which we mentioned earlier, it is necessary to carry out the conversion to more places than the decimal fraction, except in those rare cases where the decimal is equal to an exact sum of negative powers of 2, such as 0.625, for example. If we had carried out the above conversion to eight places instead of only four to the right of the binary point, we would have obtained

$$0.10010111 \ldots {}_2$$
$$= \frac{1}{2} + \frac{1}{16} + \frac{1}{64} + \frac{1}{128} + \frac{1}{256} = 0.58984_{10}$$

The error here is 0.00226, or about 0.4%. This is about the precision we can expect with a fraction expressed in only a single byte.

ELECTRICAL REPRESENTATION OF BINARY NUMBERS

It is seen that a binary number is represented as a series of ONES and ZEROES. The corresponding circuit that carries this analogue must have a corresponding series of HIGH and LOW states representing the binary number. The apparent inefficiency of the binary number system is accepted because of the simplicity and reliability of circuits that operate in only two states. A typical digital circuit operates at a nominal 5 volts for a HIGH (ONE) state and at 0.1 volt for a LOW (ZERO) state. Operation is not degraded if the HIGH state operates at 4.5 to 5.5 volts or if the LOW state operates between 0 and 1 volt. This tolerance to variation in the circuit implementation contributes to the low cost and high reliability of the digital circuit module.

All digital signal manipulations can be performed with the logical operations of AND and INVERT or NOT, which are discussed at a later point. However, from the point of view of system design and interconnection it is more efficient to think in terms of

Decoding/addressing.
Storage or memory.
Arithmetic.
Driving.

DECODING AND ADDRESSING

Decoding is the process of detecting the occurrence of a particular binary number on a particular set of interconnecting wires. A set of interconnecting wires forming a particular data pathway is generally referred to as a *bus*. Referring back to Figure 1-1, we can see that a decoder for 6, for example, would recognize the occurrence of 00110 on a five-wire bus implied for the data shown in that figure.

When a circuit element is *addressed* in a digital system, it is implied that the element has a unique number (analogous to a person's telephone number) and that there is a decoder circuit connected to respond to the unique address of the circuit element. This scheme of things is illustrated in Figure 1-2. It should be appreciated that addressing/decoding represents a very general method of communication between distinct circuit elements. The circuit elements of Figure 1-2 may represent large functions such as a printer, CRT display, or a sonic alarm, or they may represent integrated circuit elements within a larger function. The address can also refer to a place in a memory element where data or instructions are stored. In general the *decoding* function represents a many-wire (address bus) to single-wire (select) function. It should be noted that the maximum number of addresses that can be uniquely serviced from an address bus depends on the number of wires or bit positions contained in the bus. Thus a two-wire bus has only 4 unique addresses, a four-wire bus has 16 unique addresses, a five-wire bus has 32 unique addresses; in general, n wires produce 2^n addresses. The most common microprocessor address *memory* bus, as we will see, has 16 lines, hence 2^{16} or 65,536 potential locations.

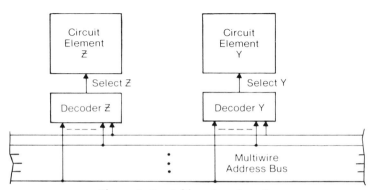

Figure 1–2   Addressing-decoding.

Storage of signal information represents one of the most significant characteristics of processor systems. Signal storage plays an important role, not only in the long term storage of data but also in the relatively short term storage of symbolic elements used by a computer such as variables, constants, and addresses of data and instructions. The two major mechanisms presently in use for storage are conveniently categorized as circuit (or solid state) and magnetic. In the early days of computer design these categories were very distinct: the two-state "flip-flop" circuit, representing the volatile or temporary storage circuit, and the magnetic core, drum or disk type representing nonvolatile mass storage techniques. (Nonvolatile storage does not lose its information when power is shut down.)

The flip-flop circuit is implemented with at least a pair of transistors connected so that when one of the transistors is switched ON the other transistor is always OFF. The circuit thus records a ONE or a ZERO depending on whether the indexed side was HIGH (OFF) or LOW (ON). The magnetic circuit depends on switching the polarity of the magnetic domains within the magnetic material for the establishment of the required two states. Functionally, these two categories of storage can be characterized by the data of Table 1-1.

These characteristics clearly dictated to early processor designs that bulk storage requirements should be met by magnetic storage techniques, while processor and system interconnecting requirements should be met with flip-flop circuit techniques.

Recent semiconductor development in the areas of MOS integrated circuit memory (memory "chips") and electrically erasable ROMs (read only memories) are beginning to blur these distinctions. At the present time individual flip-flop circuits are still used within the processor and for system interconnection requirements, but the MOS memory is beginning to find widespread use as the main memory in microprocessor systems, particularly in conjunction with nonvolatile ROM.

The *memory* function in a processor system provides an example of a

Table 1-1   Characteristics of Magnetic and Circuit Storage

Circuit Storage	Magnetic Storage
Rapid access and change	Relatively slow access and change
Higher cost per bit	Lower cost per bit
Available in small units	Economically available in large storage units
Data lost with loss of power	Nonvolatile, data retained on power loss

system unit with built-in decoding. The random access memory (RAM) connects to the processor system with three distinct busses: an address bus, a data bus, and a control bus. The RAM may be thought of as a series of stacked trays, each tray containing part of a data word. Figure 1-3 illustrates the organization of an integrated circuit memory module. Illustrated is an organization of 256 words, each word containing 4 bits of data. This organization is represented by Intel part 2101A, Motorola part 5101, or RCA part 1822D, among others. As illustrated, each such integrated circuit contains a full decoder to select one of the 256 words stored. Since 256 equals 2^8, eight lines of the address bus must connect to the decoder. The decoder is also provided with an ENABLE line which connects to an external decoder (not shown). The external decoder connects in turn to higher order address bits, and thus permits many of the units shown in Figure 1-3 to be assembled into a large memory system.

The READ/WRITE control signal shown in Figure 1-3 permits a single 4-bit *data port* to serve both the READ and the WRITE functions. The data port brings data *from* the internally addressed

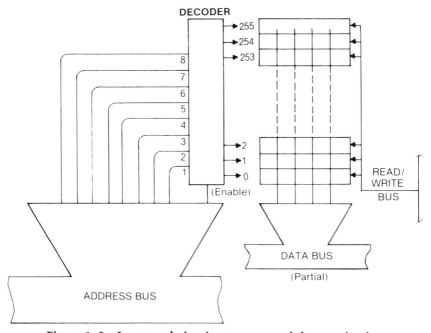

Figure 1–3   Integrated circuit memory module organization.

memory word when the control line is held in the READ state. When the control line is placed in the WRITE state, the circuit *enters* data by altering the contents of the addressed memory word in accordance with the binary data supplied to the data port by the data bus. The memory data port thus provides a bidirectional pathway for data in and out of the memory, which is fully compatible with the modern concept of the bidirectional data bus.

The READ/WRITE control signal is normally held in the READ state to prevent noise or random variations from entering the memory. The READ/WRITE control line effectively acts as a memory write strobe control. A strobe in this case is a signal that places the circuit in the WRITE state only when the memory input data is stable and noisefree. A microprocessor system generally operates on binary words of 8 or 16 bits. Integrated circuit memories are supplied with addressable word organizations that are 1, 4, or 8 bits in width. The variations are generally reflections of the state of the art in memory semiconductor processing, and reflect efforts to provide the minimum cost for memories of various total size. The first products of new memory technologies tend to provide many words, each one bit wide. As the fabrication process improves, the memory becomes available with increasingly wider words. Thus the first 1K* memories were 1 bit wide; these were followed by organizations of 1K by 4 and 1K by 8. Generally the designer is obliged to use several integrated circuit memory chips side by side to obtain the required word size.

ARITHMETIC AND LOGIC

The capability for high-speed arithmetic was the requirement that first provided the impetus for the development of the first electronic digital computers. In the binary system arithmetic functions can be carried out by using the operations of *Boolean algebra* (binary logic).

We have already seen how the binary system and its extensions, octal and hexadecimal, are used to represent integer and fractional numbers. We must now consider how the microprocessor can use the binary representation to perform the operations of arithmetic, such as ADD and SUBTRACT.

---

*K is conventionally used to refer to memory sizes of approximately 1000 words, actually 1024 words.

BINARY LOGIC AND ADDITION

The rules for adding single bits are very simple and can be summarized as follows:

Augend		Addend		Sum	
0	+	0	=	0	
0	+	1	=	1	
1	+	0	=	1	
1	+	1	=	0	(carry neglected)

The complication arises when more than 1 bit is used, that is, when the carry is considered. The carry, of course, is the 1 that must be carried to the next higher order of bits when we add $1 + 1$.

A logical blackbox that accounts for both sum and carry is shown in Figure 1-4.

The reason for the term *half adder* is that only the outgoing carry is accounted for, not one that could enter from a lower order blackbox. As we will see, two half adders are needed to complete the additional task.

The rules for specifying the output of the half adder as a function of its inputs can be put in the form shown in Table 1-2. Such a table is known as a *truth table* in binary logic. Note that all four of the possible combinations of A and B (where either can be 0 or 1) are specified as inputs. The sum output is the same as for single bit addition, and the carry to the next higher order of bits occurs only when both inputs are 1's.

LOGIC ELEMENTS

To see how such a blackbox can be constructed, we must first define the elements of binary logic. These are the basic building blocks of binary arithmetic. Actually, there are a great many possible logic elements that we can use as basic ones. For all combinations of two inputs, such as A

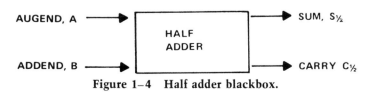

Figure 1–4   Half adder blackbox.

Table 1-2   Half Adder Truth Table

Augend, A	Addend, B	Sum, $S_{1/2}$	Carry, $C_{1/2}$
0	0	0	0
1	0	1	0
0	1	1	0
1	1	0	1

and B in Table 1-2, there are 16 different possible output combinations, including those shown in the half adder sum and carry columns. Some of these 16 are trivial; for example, the output can always be 0 regardless of the values of A and B, or it can always be 1. Two of these elementary logic functions are intuitively considered basic, and all other functions can be built up from these. They are AND and OR (nonexclusive). The AND function can be symbolized by a multiplication sign (dot) (Figure 1-5). Its truth table is

A	B	$A \cdot B$ (AND)
0	0	0
1	0	0
0	1	0
1	1	1

In accordance with its name, the AND function is true (1) only when A and B are 1. Otherwise it is false, or 0.

The AND function can be easily envisioned as two switches in series, as shown in the Figure 1-5. The lamp, $A \cdot B$ will light only if both A and B switches are closed. You can readily convince yourself that the circuit will obey the truth table for AND, if you assume that a closed switch or a lighted lamp means 1 and the converse means 0. Obviously, semiconductor switches are substituted in the logic elements of the integrated circuits, but the principle is the same.

The nonexclusive OR is also intuitively logical. Its symbol is the + sign (see Figure 1-6), and its truth table is

A	B	$A + B$ (OR)
0	0	0
1	0	1
0	1	1
1	1	1

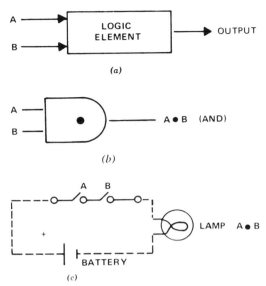

Figure 1–5   General logic and AND elements.

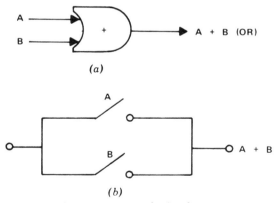

Figure 1–6   OR logic element.

The OR function is true if either A or B is true, and is 0 (false) only if neither is true. An embodiment of an OR element consists of two parallel switches, as shown in Figure 1-6. By connecting this assembly of switches to the lamp and battery circuit, you can assure yourself that it obeys the logical or truth table as well as the analogous circuit in the AND case.

With the addition of one more logical concept, that of NOT, or complementation, we can build up any of the 16 logic functions. NOT is merely the negation or inversion of a single variable. It is symbolized by an overbar, as in $\bar{A}$, or by a circle in a block diagram, and can be envisioned as a one-stage (inverting) amplifier or a normally open relay closed by means of an external circuit (Figure 1-7).

The truth table for NOT is simply

A	$\bar{A}$
0	1
1	0

With these three logic elements, AND, OR, and NOT, we can achieve all the possible two-input logic functions, including the half adder sum and carry. (Actually, there are two even more fundamental functions, the NOR or not-OR, called the *Pierce function*, and the NAND or not-AND, also known as the *Sheffer stroke*.) The NOR and the NAND (Figure 1-8) functions are most commonly used in practical integrated circuitry, but are more complex to show as examples of implementation.

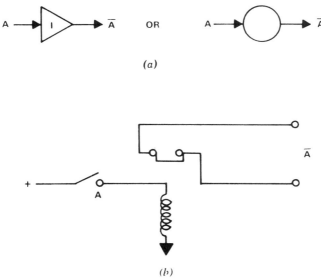

Figure 1–7   NOT logic element.

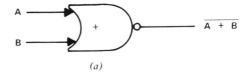

$$(a)$$

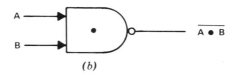

$$(b)$$

Figure 1–8   NOR (*a*) and NAND (*b*) logic elements.

HALF ADDER IMPLEMENTATION

Even restricting ourselves to the AND, OR, and NOT elements, there are a great many embodiments of the half adder truth table. Only one is shown here (Figure 1-9).

To prove that this is indeed a half adder, we need merely construct its truth table. Note that the inputs to the $S\frac{1}{2}$ AND element are D, the output of the OR, and E, the negation of the input AND (thus E is really a NAND of A and B). Thus we can construct Table 1-3 from the possible A and B inputs. Now, comparing the $S\frac{1}{2}$ and $C\frac{1}{2}$ columns of Table 1-3 with those of Table 1-2, we see they are identical; therefore the circuit shown is a half adder.

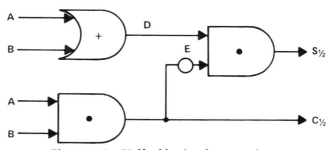

Figure 1–9   Half adder implementation.

Table 1-3   Proof of Half Adder Logic

A	B	D	$C\frac{1}{2}$	E	$S\frac{1}{2}$
		$A + B$	$A \cdot B$	$\overline{A \cdot B}$	$D \cdot E$
0	0	0	0	1	0
1	0	1	0	1	1
0	1	1	0	1	1
1	1	1	1	0	0

We could also show the properties of the circuit by manipulating the logical equations (Boolean algebra). From Figure 1-9 we can see that

$$S\frac{1}{2} = D \cdot E$$

but

$$D = A + B$$

and

$$E = \overline{A \cdot B}$$

Two basic theorems of Boolean algebra (which you can prove by constructing truth tables) are

$$\overline{A \cdot B} = \overline{A} + \overline{B} \qquad \text{(deMorgan's theorem)}$$

and

$$X \cdot \overline{X} = 0$$

From deMorgan's theorem, we can conclude that

$$E = \overline{A} + \overline{B}$$

and

$$S\frac{1}{2} = (A + B) \cdot (\overline{A} + \overline{B})$$

Multiplying out the terms (omitting the dots), we obtain

$$S\frac{1}{2} = A\overline{A} + A\overline{B} + B\overline{B} + B\overline{A}$$

and, dropping zero terms, $\overline{A}$ and $B\overline{B} = 0$,

$$S\frac{1}{2} = A\overline{B} + B\overline{A}$$

This function is called the *exclusive OR* and has the following truth table:

A	B	$A\bar{B} + B\bar{A}$
0	0	0
1	0	1
0	1	1
1	1	0

which is identical to the sum $S_{1/2}$. The carry $C_{1/2}$ is merely the AND function of the inputs $C_{1/2} = A \cdot B$, as shown in Figure 1-9.

FULL ADDER IMPLEMENTATION

Having developed the logic circuitry for the half adder, we go to the full adder, which will permit us to perform all the required digital arithmetic operations. The full adder has three inputs, the augend and addend bits, as in the half adder, plus a carry bit from the *previous* stage of the adder. The outputs are a sum bit, which is obtained by applying the rules for adding single bits (with no carry) to all three inputs, and a carry bit to the next stage. There is a carry bit C if at least two of the input bits are 1's. Therefore the full adder can be cascaded for any number of stages to achieve any desired accuracy in terms of binary digit representation of a number.

The truth table for a full adder is shown in Table 1-4.

Figure 1-10 shows a possible implementation of a full adder using half adder (exclusive-OR) logic. Note that this is only one of the many

Table 1-4   Full Adder Truth Table

A	B	C	S	C_1
0	0	0	0	0
1	0	0	1	0
0	1	0	1	0
1	1	0	0	1
0	0	1	1	0
1	0	1	0	1
0	1	1	0	1
1	1	1	1	1

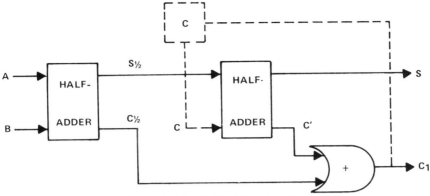

Figure 1–10   Full adder circuit.

possible circuits that can be used to implement this function. However, the choice of the chip designer will not concern us in our application of the microprocessor as long as we comprehend the principles involved.

SUBTRACTION AND NEGATIVE NUMBERS

It is possible to design special circuitry to perform the subtraction operation using the same logical methods as for addition, but it is obviously more efficient to be able to perform both operations using the same hardware. Fortunately this can be accomplished by substituting for a subtraction algorithm the equivalent operation of *algebraic addition*, that is, adding two numbers, one of which has been made negative. Therefore it is now necessary to discuss the concept of *negative number*.

Any negative quantity can be considered positive from a different point of view; for example, $-10°C$ is positive on the Fahrenheit scale, and a debit is a credit on someone else's books. In digital calculating machines negative numbers are a bother, since a counting device must sense 0 and also be able to operate in both directions; thus

$$3$$
$$2$$
$$1$$
$$0$$
$$-1$$
$$-2$$

If a counter is so arranged that some positive numbers substitute for the negatives, the complexity of zero sensing and direction changing can be avoided. For example,

$$
\begin{array}{rcl}
+\,2 & \text{is represented by} & 0002 \\
1 & \text{by} & 0001 \\
0 & \text{by} & 0000 \\
-\,1 & \text{by} & 9999 \\
-\,2 & \text{by} & 9998 \\
& \text{and so on} &
\end{array}
$$

This notation is known as *10's complements;* actually only the least significant digit is 10's complemented (subtracted from 10) to obtain the value of the negative number; the remaining digits are really 9's complemented. If we restrict the capacity of the counter to the range $+8999$ to -1000, the digit 9 in the most significant place can be used to indicate the sign of the balance; for example, 9 acts as the minus sign.

2's Complement Form

In a similar way we can define a negative binary number by using a 2's complement. The rules for forming a 2's complement are as follows.

POSITIVE NUMBER

Append a binary 0 above the highest order magnitude bit as a + sign and keep the magnitude bits unchanged.

Example: Binary 5   = 0101
           2's complement form   = 00101

NEGATIVE NUMBER

Append a binary 1 above the highest order magnitude bit as a − sign and replace the magnitude bits as follows (2's complement): (1) Replace all 1's by 0's, and vice versa (1's complement); (2) Add 1. Ignore any further carry out caused by the addition.

Example: Binary minus 7 $= -\;0111$
    1's complement   1000
    Add 1 $+\quad\;\;1$

                                   1001
    Add minus sign bit   11001

Assuming that we have 8 binary places or the equivalent 2 hexadecimal (8 bits), we can convert the 256 possible positive numbers (including zero) as follows:

Hexadecimal	Binary	Decimal
00	00000000	0
01	00000001	1
02	00000010	2
	•	
	•	
	•	
FE	11111110	254
FF	11111111	255

to 128 positive and 128 negative numbers, by using the 2's complement. Thus we obtain the following table:

00	00000000	0
01	00000001	+1
	•	
	•	
	•	
7F	01111111	+127
FF	11111111	−1
FE	11111110	−2
Fd	11111101	−3
	•	
	•	
	•	
80	10000000	−128

Negative numbers can always be converted to positive ones by reapplying the 2's complement operation; that is, convert the 1's to 0's and vice versa, then add 1. The most significant (leftmost) bit is then always the sign bit. If it is a 1, the number is negative; if it is a zero, the number is positive. Of course, by using one of the 8 bits for this purpose we have lost half the range of the unsigned bits. That is, with 8 bits we can only count to -128 or $+127$ instead of the unsigned value of 256.

To see how the signed binary 2's complement can be used for subtraction, consider the problem of taking the difference between two fractions, first using ordinary arithmetic implemented by an imaginary "subtractor" circuit.

		Decimal Equivalent
A +	0.1001001	0.57013125_{10}
B −	0.0110000	0.375_{10}
+	0.0011001_{2}	0.1953125_{10}

Now, using the rules specified for 2's complement, we can convert the negative number B and add, obtaining the same result:

0.0110000	$+B$ (subtrahend)
0.1001111	1's complement of B
1	Add initial carry (1)
0.1010000	2's complement of B
1.1010000	Add minus sign bit for $-B$
0.1001001	Add $+A$
10.0011001	$A - B$
0.0011001	Throw away extra carry

The answer is the same as before, and neither the hardware nor the rules must be changed, other than to 2's complement the subtrahend.

In the event that the subtrahend is larger than the minuend, the sum is negative, and the result N is in 2's complement form $(2^n - N)$. Although this is satisfactory for the machine, for external representation, if magnitude and sign are displayed separately, the result must be again complemented, since $2^n - (2^n - N) = N$.

To subtract 8 from 3 in complement form, we proceed as follows:

1000	Binary 8
0111	1's complement
1	Initial carry
11000	Add sign bit (binary -8)
00011	Binary $+3$

$$11011 \quad \text{Result, 2's complement}$$
$$0100$$
$$\underline{1}$$
$$1\ \underbrace{0101}\quad \text{Recomplemented result}$$

$$-\ \text{Sign}\quad \text{Magnitude 5}$$

HIGHER ARITHMETIC FUNCTIONS

We have spent a great deal of time on the addition function because it is fundamental to all other binary arithmetic. Once we are able to add and handle negative numbers (subtract), all other operations can be performed with only a few minor embellishments. For example, the act of multiplication is merely repeated addition, and that of division merely subtraction.

In a microcomputer most or all of the higher functions are performed by instructions, or programs, which are orders to control the sequence of basic operations. In older computers these instructions were called *software routines*, and were selected by the programmer as part of the overall process of setting up a particular job on the computer. In a microcomputer these instructions are usually put into *firmware*, which amounts to a permanent memory (read only memory, ROM), which becomes an integral part of the computer.

Although we could multiply by repeated addition of the multiplicand controller by a *counter*, together with some means to detect when the count reached the value of the multiplier, in practice this would be quite slow, and there are easier ways to accomplish it. The basic binary multiplication table is quite simple, and there are no carries to complicate things.

		Multiplicand digit	
		0	1
Multiplier digit	0	0	0
	1	0	1

Therefore it pays to use the logic in the table and to multiply by the rote method taught to children:

```
Multiplicand   0.11101
Multiplier      0.11110    Multiplier digit
                  00000          0
                  11101          1
                  11101          1
                  11101          1
                  11101          1
              0.1101100110
```

We have introduced one new concept here, that of *shift*. As each higher order multiplier digit is utilized, the partial product is shifted one binary place to the left. A shift of the partial product to the left, or of the binary point to the right, is equivalent to multiplication by 2, just as shifting the decimal point in base 10 notation is equivalent to multiplication by 10.

If you attempt to follow through the above multiplication, you will encounter one more difficulty—summing the partial products. This is because there are both single and multiple carries in the addition, and it is difficult to keep them straight. In machine implementation one usually accumulates the partial products as one goes along, although not for the same reason. The machine calculation would then look like this:

```
                  0.11101      Accumulated
        X         0.11110      Partial Product     Multiplier digit
                   00000
                   00000                                  0
                   00000          x
                   11101                                  1
                  111010          x
                   11101                                  1
                 10101110         x
                  11101                                  1
                110010110         x
                 11101                                   1
Product      0.1101100110        x
```

If the two numbers being multiplied are *signed*, there are rules of some complexity involving 2's complements, but the above is sufficient to show the principles of multiplication.

Note, however, that this is only one of several methods available. There are others that the designer may choose to incorporate in the firmware. There are several ways of performing *division*. The method of *trial division* is one of the more popular. In this method the divisor is compared with the remainder. If the divisor is greater than the remainder, no subtraction is actually performed and a 0 is placed in the lowest order of the quotient. If the divisor is not greater than the remainder, it is subtracted from the remainder and a 1 bit is placed in the quotient. After each quotient bit is calculated, the dividend is shifted and the loop repeated (see Ref. 2).

Negative numbers introduce slight complications to these schemes. Furthermore, the divisor must be greater than the dividend (the quotient is less than 1) for most routines.

DRIVING

Driving is the process of activating the various wires that electrically interconnect the physical elements of the processor system. The speed at which data words are switched in the modern processor necessitates that the problems of driving the signal wires be given special attention. The three major problems associated with driving computer busses are

Capacitive loading.
Signal crosstalk.
Ringing.

Electrical capacitance is associated with all physical structures. Capacitance between a signal wire and its surroundings represents a high frequency load on the circuit that is driving the wire. Unfortunately this current load increases with increasing frequency. The effect is to slow down the rate at which the signal can change state. To avoid undue slowdown, the driving circuit must be provided with sufficient overdrive capability to drive the capacitive load (at the required speed) as well as the explicit system load. The faster that the signals are being transmitted, the greater is the overdrive capability that must be provided in the driving circuit. Techniques to reduce the capacitive load are

Reduction in signal speed.
Shortening the length of the cable being driven.
Spacing signal wires away from other structures.

The preferred approach has been to reduce the signal speed on long cables, while making high speed interconnections very short and providing driving circuits with high capacitive capabilities. *Crosstalk*, another problem associated with rapidly changing signals, consists of the spurious signals coupled onto a signal wire from nearby signal wires. The coupling mechanism is that of both capacitive and inductive coupling. The effect of crosstalk is that of noise. The inherent noise immunity of digital circuits allows tolerance of some crosstalk. However, the appearance of crosstalk on a lead always reduces the amount of additional noise that can be tolerated. Crosstalk, like capacitive loading, appears because of the occurrence of distributed inductive and capacitive characteristics in the transmission wires. As the frequency components of the signals increase, the crosstalk problems become more severe. Techniques to reduce crosstalk noise include

Reduction in signal speed.
Reduction in the length of the cable receiving the noise.
Shielding.
Physical separation.

Shielding of the transmission bus represents a very effective and widely used technique for minimizing crosstalk. Shielding involves surrounding each transmission wire with a conductive cover that is connected to a ground. A coaxial cable provides a prime example of a shielded wire that will have virtually no crosstalk to parallel signal paths. Coaxial cable provides nearly 100% shielding. A somewhat lower percentage of shielding will generally provide satisfactory isolation for digital signal transmissions.

The convenience and economy of mass termination techniques has made flat (ribbon) cable a preferred interconnection medium. Basic shielding is provided in this flat cable by connection of every other wire to ground, the signals being carried on the intervening wires. A still higher level of shielding is obtained by using a flat cable having a ground shield built into the cable. This type of construction is illustrated in Figure 1-11. As shown, the ground shield is a wire mesh built into one side of the cable. The use of the ground shield, along with alternate wires connected to the ground, provides a transmission bus with characteristics approaching that of a coaxial cable.

Ringing is the tendency of a cable to show an oscillation immediately after a rapid change in state of the signal. This oscillation is due to the excitation of the resonant circuit formed by the distributed capacitance

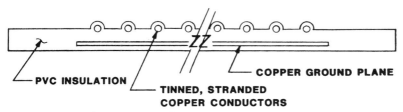

PVC INSULATION

COPPER GROUND PLANE

TINNED, STRANDED
COPPER CONDUCTORS

Figure 1–11   Shielded Flat Signal Cable.

and inductance associated with the signal wire. If uncontrolled, ringing can be a very serious interconnection problem causing the digital modules to receive spurious or unsynchronized data.

The technically correct method of handling ringing is to avoid the problem by terminating the transmission line with resistive loads that are equal to the characteristic impedance of the line. For cable systems used with microprocessor systems this characteristic impedance is usually in the range of 75 to 150 ohms. It should be appreciated that a substantial part of the power supplied by a line driver is consumed by the line terminators. As a practical matter line terminators are usually set between 150 and 330 ohms. Relatively small deviations from the optimum characteristic impedance value result in only short transient overshoots that quickly damp out. The expected appearance of spurious transients at the time of data transitions indicates the wisdom of sampling (strobing) the data after the spurious signals associated with the data transition have been damped. Such sampling is usually accomplished by using a system clock pulse or a special strobe signal.

The building of a microprocessor computer system is closely allied to the overall design of the system. The availability of large scale integrated circuit functions permits the hardware assembly of the system to closely parallel the paper block diagrams of the system.

The technology of large scale integrated circuits has resulted in the production of major system functions in the form of a single circuit component. This situation highlights the emphasis of this book on the interface and communication between the various circuit elements of the system. Defining these interfaces in lesser and greater detail defines both the system function and the details of wiring. A basic microprocessor system can be implemented with just two basic functions: a microprocessor and a memory. This basic system illustrates a simple and yet perhaps most profound characteristic of a processor based system, the concept of interfacing or communicating between discrete entities by addressing. By giving each discrete element a unique address, a large number of elements can be interconnected over a small communication channel. This concept was seen applied above to the workings of an integrated memory circuit (Figure 1-3). It was seen that the basic idea can be readily expanded through the use of address decoding (on the higher order address lines) to include a large number of parallel memory circuits.

TIMING

A specially designed logic chip using high speed bipolar technology can perform arithmetic operations such as the addition of two 4-bit numbers (present at the inputs) within 10 to 25 nanoseconds. However, in a typical microprocessor one or more clock periods (cycles) are required to perform each of several tasks required for the entire operation, such as fetch an address from memory or add. A complete arithmetic operation therefore requires several cycles. For example, the pioneer 4-bit MOS microprocessor, the Intel 4004, required 8 or 16 cycles of 750-kilohertz clock time, or 10.6 to 21.3 microseconds, for a basic operation. The General Instrument CP-1600, which uses the relatively fast n-channel MOS technology, has a clock cycle time of 400 nanoseconds and requires 3.2 microseconds to add two 16-bit numbers. Similarly the LSI-11 of Digital Equipment Corporation requires 3.5 to 4.2 microseconds to add, 24 to 64 to multiply, and a worst case of 78 microseconds for a 16-bit divide.

In a microprocessor a complex process such as division or multiplication is usually not available as a single instruction, and is programmed from the more basic instructions in a set; for example, a divide routine used with the General Instrument Company CP-1600 requires 13 instructions iterated once per bit.

2

Microprocessors

The digital processor or central processing unit (CPU), first as the minicomputer and now in the form called *microprocessor*, has become the preeminent all-purpose electronic control unit. The hierarchy of digital computers, with processing speeds ranging from those of the super giants, aimed at manipulating large matrix equations, to that of the smallest integrated circuit microprocessor used in a toy, is linked by a set of common ideas. These common threads include an implementation based on binary (2-state) logic, the use of basic logic elements: AND gates, OR gates, and inverters; a stored instruction or control sequence; and the use of addressing to control communication routes between the devices of a system. All processors have the ability to *fetch* (obtain from memory) and execute a limited set of instructions, to perform addition and subtraction on a binary word, and to input (take in) and output (put out) binary data. In many situations the processor has many more capabilities than the application requires. However, the cost efficiencies of standardized mass production usually makes the use of an overqualified processor preferable to the construction of specialized logic units.

PROGRAM PREPARATION

Computers operate from a list of instructions expressed in binary form known as the *program*. The program list is initially generated by the human programmer and entered into the computer memory. The basic process is shown in Figure 2-1.

There are two methods by which the program can enter the computer. As we have seen, the CPU only understands binary code. The

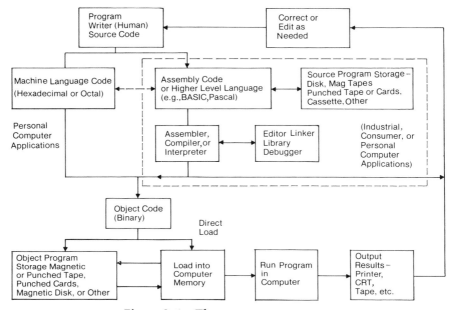

Figure 2–1   The computer process.

human programmer must first prepare the program, known as the *source code.*

If he prepares this in binary (or the equivalent hexadecimal or octal, which is immediately convertible to binary), this program also becomes the binary *object code* which is understood by the computer. But machine language is very difficult for humans to remember and use without mistakes. It is much easier to write a program using an *assembly language* which features a *structure* such as mnemonics, or code names resembling natural language, that help the programmer to recall their meaning. For example, it is much easier to remember that ADC means "add with carry" than to recall 01101101, the binary, or 6D, the hexadecimal equivalent (in the 6502 microprocessor.) So-called *higher level* languages such as BASIC, FORTRAN, Pascal, and COBOL are designed to match even more closely the programmer's thought processes and to have more structure in the form of syntax (grammar), other rules, and redundancy, which reduce coding errors. Although $C = A + B$ is even more readily understood than the assembly equivalent,

LDA (load from memory location).

ADC (add with carry).

STA (store in memory).

the latter is a definite improvement over an unstructured binary sequence of 1's and 0's.

The alternative path to object code shown, in Figure 2-1, is through assembly or higher level languages, using the blocks shown enclosed in the dashed box. It is also possible, as shown, for the programmer to code in assembly language and then hand-convert to hexadecimal/object code, since there is a one-to-one relationship between them. In fact, this is the path taken by many personal computer owners. The more professional way, which is invariably chosen by developers of industrial instruments or consumer products using microprocessors, is to write source code in assembly or a higher level language, and automatically (using a computer) translate this into binary object code. This involves other programs (for the translating computer), known as *assemblers* for assembly language, or *compilers* or *interpreters* for higher level languages. These programs are of considerable complexity and require a good deal of memory and operating time, but this operation need not be conducted on the microcomputer for which the program is designed. Professionally sophisticated systems (*development systems*) are used for the program development and may be minicomputers or even time-share facilities on very large computers. Other, even more sophisticated programs are used to help the programmer. These include *editors*, which permit correction of program errors, additions, and deletions; *linkers*, which assemble several programs and assign memory locations; and *libraries* of frequently used programs or *subroutines* which may be named and called on by the programmer rather than rewritten each time they are used.

The purpose of all these facilities is to save the programmer's time and money, since software development is clearly the biggest cost in microprocessor applications today. This same motivation applies to the use of easily understood and logically structured high level languages (such as Pascal) rather than machine or assembly code, since the most invariable and costly part of software development is *debugging* or elimination or errors from the program. (Some development systems have special programs, called *debuggers*, to aid in correcting errors. The significance of this correction process is shown in Figure 2-1 by the feedback path, following the loading and running of the program and output of results, back to the programmer for correction as required. It is a rare program that does not require several of these iterations during its development. The compilers, debuggers, and so on, are also designed to send helpful messages to the human programmer whenever they detect errors.

Home computer operators may have some of these facilities, although usually in less elaborate form than in professional development systems. For example, the most rudimentary form of the SYM-1 (a 6502 microprocessor board) accepts hexadecimal directly through a keyboard, which is one step below assembly language, but permits direct inspection and change of memory locations. It even produces very rudimentary error messages, all using an editor-operating system called a *monitor* (SUPERMON). BASIC and other high level languages, together with editors of various types, can be purchased for most home microcomputers, either as software or as ROM firmware.

Because of the volatile nature of the RAM memory, where user programs are stored (the programs are lost when power is removed and must then be reentered), it is necessary to store the latter in some nonvolatile medium such as magnetic disk or tape, punched tape, or card. Professional equipment stores source programs for the duration of the development process and documentation (future modification or error correction) because the source program is the most comprehensible to a human programmer and the modifier may not be the original author. Both professional and home computer users need to store the object program if it is ever to be rerun because of memory volatility. The home user who invests in the minimum of equipment can use the computer itself to transfer his or her program to a conventional audio tape cassette. (The SYM-1 mentioned earlier has a program included in its monitor which converts a block of object code in memory to *serial* form—discussed in the next chapter—and output to an audio recorder through a simple interface included on the board.) This use of the CPU for direct output to a slow peripheral such as a tape cassette recorder is very inefficient and time consuming, and would never be tolerated in a large computer environment. However, the personal computer is very affordable whereas additional equipment such as disk drives is expensive, so this method makes sense in its context.

PROCESSOR ROLE

After a program has been loaded into the computer, it is run on command of the computer operator. The end result of any program is the *output* that it effects. This computer output must be applied to some specialized device, such as a CRT screen, a printer, a motor, or a relay to make it sensible to humans. Sometimes the specialized device is a steel furnace or a guided missile.

Internally, the computer is comprised of a number of specialized circuit functions and electrical pathways or gates providing interconnections between these circuits. Each object program code word received by the computer is decoded to provide and execute a sequence of internal micro-operations involving these specialized circuits. The micro sequence of operations is commonly called the *operation code* or *op code*. The reader will notice a hierarchy of coding in computer technology. Specific gates within the computer are enabled by a decoded microinstruction. The microinstruction results from decoding an op code, and the op code is obtained by decoding a particular memory address where a word of the computer program is stored. And, as we have already noted, in the simplest form of computer systems the programmer writes his program as a series of op codes, while in more sophisticated systems the program is written in a high-level language such as BASIC. In general, each line of program instruction in a high-level language is decoded or interpreted as a sequence of op codes. It should be noted that a source program written in a high-level language (such as BASIC) can be run on many different processor systems provided, or course, that the systems are equipped with an appropriate compiler or interpreter to handle the language. Thus the high-level languages represent a more generalized approach to programming.

A very large number of processors are now available. In the larger computers the CPU is always unique to a particular manufacturer. The integrated circuit microprocessors, however, usually have several sources for each type and are known by a code number analogous to the code numbers assigned to transistors and other components. Some of the most widely used microprocessors are members of families designated by the codes Z-80, 6800, and 6500. Microprocessors are usually classified with regard to data word size (e.g., 4-bit, 8-bit, or 16-bit), the semiconductor technology type with which the microprocessor is implemented, and the size of the address word that the microprocessor uses. These coarse characterizations are useful because the implications of each category relate to the ultimate use of the processor. For efficient processing the data word size should be closely attuned to the number of bits needed to describe the data that will be coming into the processor and to the data size that will be used by devices receiving data from the processor. Processors can manipulate word sizes larger than the size of their own internal word, but at the cost of a significant amount of extra instruction steps.

The semiconductor technology with which a microprocessor is implemented implies several attributes of the processor. An implementation in *CMOS* technology implies a very low power requirement, high noise immunity, tolerance of a wide range of power supply voltages, and modest clock speed. *NMOS* technology implies intermediate speed and power characteristics and relatively high-density (complex circuit potential) circuitry. *Bipolar* technology implies very high speed, relatively high power requirements, and low circuit density, which usually means multiple circuit packages (chips) are needed to implement a processor. The size of the address word indicates the maximum amount of program memory (RAM or ROM) that can be accommodated by the processor. It also can indicate the relative ease with which nonmemory devices can be connected to the processor, since unused higher order memory bit positions can be employed in place of input/output device decoders.

MICROPROCESSOR ARCHITECTURE

The fundamental element of microprocessor architecture is the *register*. A register is used for temporary storage of digital data and can have a capacity ("width") from 1 bit to 16 bits. It is used to store a word or part of a word of binary data. Conceptually a register is similar to a single word of memory. Data are transferred into the register, and the data remain in the register (as long as power is maintained on the device) until new data are transferred in, at which time the new data supersede the old data. Circuitry connected to each bit of the register uses the register's data continuously until the processor calls for a change. A register differs from a memory word in that it is not necessary to address the register to access its data. The mere presence of the data in the register is assurance that it is available for use.

Figure 2-2 shows in outline the generalized architecture of a basic microprocessor. The major elements shown are

Program counter.
Accumulator register.
Arithmetic and logic unit.
Instruction register.
Timing control.

The *program counter* is a counting register that, when pulsed, adds 1 to its present value. The program counter is used to address the memory for fetching each successive op code of the program being executed. After fetching an op code from the program in memory, while this operation is being executed, the program counter is automatically incremented by one unit. At the completion of the instruction, it is then ready with the address for the following program instruction. The simplicity of the program counter function is based on the convention that

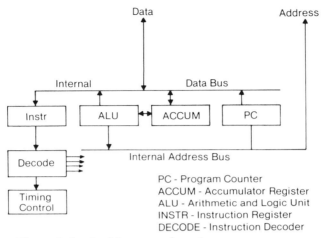

Figure 2–2   Architecture of a microprocessor.

the successive program instructions are always stored in the memory in ascending order at adjacent memory addresses. Note that with this scheme of things it is only necessary to initially set the program counter to a value representing the address of the first instruction of the program. During the running of a computer program, there usually is a point where the program branches to an auxiliary list of stored instructions. The branch is effected by setting into the program counter a new number representing the branch address corresponding to the starting address of the auxiliary list. Setting of the program counter to a branch address during execution is called a *branch* or *jump* type of op code. Thus at the completion of such an instruction the program counter value is used in the normal way as the address for fetching the next instruction code; however, since the program counter value was changed during the execution of the branch instruction, the next op code is fetched from the beginning of the new and nonadjacent sequence that it was designed to execute. As the block diagram of Figure 2-2 shows, the internal data bus of the processor connects to the program counter, as well as to all of the other internal registers of the processor. In a branch operation the new value for the program counter is received from memory into an internal register and, during execution of the branch instruction, set into the program counter. The specific source for the value that is set into the program counter depends on the addressing mode of the particular instruction being executed.

The *accumulator register* is a simple storage register designed primarily to work in conjunction with the *arithmetic and logic unit* (ALU). The main purpose of the accumulator is to receive data from the ALU and to provide data input to the ALU.

The ALU is the section of the processor where the data manipulation is done. It is here that the functions of addition, subtraction, shifting, and comparison are performed. The arithmetic and comparison functions require two data inputs; the accumulator register provides one input, while the second one is applied to the ALU over the data bus. Conventionally, the ALU has no storage of its own, but relies on the storage provided by the data bus (memory, for example) and the accumulator.

The *instruction register* receives and stores the op code while it is being executed by the processor. The *instruction decoder* circuitry receives the op code data from the instruction register and generates the appropriate decoded signal. Signal sequences are then generated, as required by the op code, through the interaction of the decoded op code signal with the timing control signals. The result of all of these interactions is the automatic receipt, transfer, and manipulation of the digital signals dictated by the specification of the corresponding op code.

Although each op code of the processor's instruction set is necessarily unique, the initial sequence of operations involved in the processing of a program instruction is common to all computers. When a computer starts to run a program, it must initially fetch the instruction from memory and enter the instruction into the instruction register. To fetch the instruction, the following sequence of micro operations must occur:

1   Gate the value of the program counter onto the address bus.
2   Generate a strobe (action) signal to enter the instruction obtained from the addressed memory into the instruction register.
3   Decode the op code residing in the instruction register and initiate the series of timing signals that, in conjunction with the decoded instruction signal, will execute the required instruction.
4   Increment the program counter one unit to prepare it for its next operation. At this point in the operation, the internal events of the processor become unique to the particular instruction.

It should be noted that different instructions require varying numbers of processor clock cycle times to complete, the more complex instructions requiring the longer intervals for completion.

MICROPROCESSOR EXAMPLE—6502

In this section we examine a microprocessor that is representative of the 8-bit microprocessors that are now generally available. We consider in detail the 6502 microprocessor, a member of the 6500 family. The processor utilizes a memory address that is 16 bits wide, has an 8-bit data word, and is fabricated with NMOS semiconductor technology. The 16-bit address gives it a capability of addressing up to 65,536 memory words; the 8-bit data word indicates that it can efficiently handle numeric and alphabetical characters and that it will have to employ multiple precision (multiword) programming for almost all numeric data processing. The NMOS semiconductor technology implies a medium speed device; the 6500 series processors are available with maximum clock frequencies of 1, 2, and 3 million cycles per second.

The architecture of the 6500 series microprocessor, shown in Figure 2-3, is generally similar to the basic architecture shown in Figure 2-2, in that the same elements are present and the 6500 design also is built around a data bus; however, in this design the data bus is strictly internal to the package. Figure 2-3 shows a number of additional elements that supplement the basic design already considered. Within the microprocessor package the individual transistors operate at extremely low current levels, implying that they have a very low capability to charge any external capacity as they switch between HIGH and LOW states. Therefore, the external load capacity must be isolated from the internal microprocessor circuits by input and output buffer circuits. The 6502 address bus is buffered through ABL, the lower 8 bits (byte) of the address, and ABH, the high byte or upper 8 address bits. Similarly, the external data bus is isolated through the data bus buffer. For economic reasons the general strategy of the 8-bit microprocessor design is to minimize the required pin count of the microprocessor package (chip). This is done through utilization of the 16-bit address bus and the bidirectional 8-bit data bus. Input data from the external data bus transfers into the instruction register and the data latch (DL) at times appropriate to the internal operation of the microprocessor. As indicated, the instruction data is used only for instruction decoding. General input data can be transferred from the data latch to the internal data bus of the processor and thus transferred to any of the processor's data manipulating functions.

The program counter is the only 16-bit register within the "8-bit" microprocessor. It is broken into two 8-bit sections to conveniently

SY6500 INTERNAL ARCHITECTURE

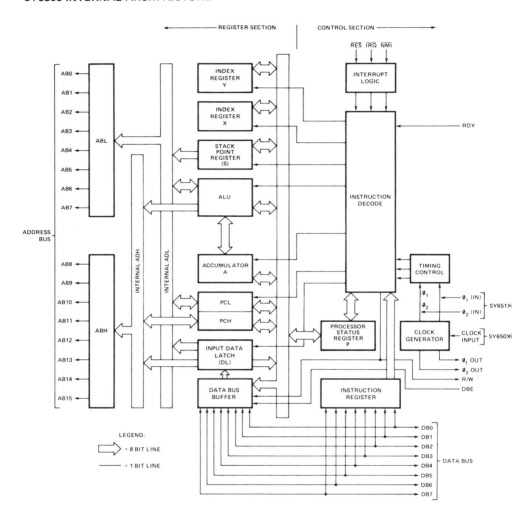

NOTE:
1. CLOCK GENERATOR IS NOT INCLUDED ON SY651X.
2. ADDRESSING CAPABILITY AND CONTROL OPTIONS VARY WITH
   EACH OF THE SY6500 PRODUCTS.

42

PIN FUNCTIONS

Clocks ($\emptyset_1$, $\emptyset_2$)

The SY651X requires a two phase non-overlapping clock that runs at the V_{CC} voltage level.

The SY650X clocks are supplied with an internal clock generator. The frequency of these clocks is externally controlled. Clock generator circuits are shown elsewhere in this data sheet.

Address Bus (A_0-A_{15}) (See sections on each micro for respective address lines on those devices.)

These outputs are TTL compatible, capable of driving one standard TTL load and 130 pF.

Data Bus (DB_0-DB_7)

Eight pins are used for the data bus. This is a bi-directional bus, transferring data to and from the device and peripherals. The outputs are three-state buffers, capable of driving one standard TTL load and 130 pF.

Data Bus Enable (DBE)

This TTL compatible input allows external control of the three-state data output buffers and will enable the microprocessor bus driver when in the high state. In normal operation DBE would be driven by the phase two ($\emptyset_2$) clock, thus allowing data output from microprocessor only during $\emptyset_2$. During the read cycle, the data bus drivers are internally disabled, becoming essentially an open circuit. To disable data bus drivers externally, DBE should be held low. This signal is available on the SY6512, only.

Ready (RDY)

This input signal allows the user to halt the microprocessor on all cycles except write cycles. A negative transition to the low state during or coincident with phase one ($\emptyset_1$) will halt the microprocessor with the output address lines reflecting the current address being fetched. This condition will remain through a subsequent phase two ($\emptyset_2$) in which the Ready signal is low. This feature allows microprocessor interfacing with low speed PROMS as well as fast (max. 2 cycle) Direct Memory Access (DMA). If ready is low during a write cycle, it is ignored until the following read operation. Ready transitions must not be permitted during $\emptyset_2$ time.

Interrupt Request ($\overline{IRQ}$)

This TTL level input requests that an interrupt sequence begin within the microprocessor. The microprocessor will complete the current instruction being executed before recognizing the request. At that time, the interrupt mask bit in the Status Code Register will be examined. If the interrupt mask flag is not set, the microprocessor will begin an interrupt sequence. The Program Counter and Processor Status Register are stored in the stack. The microprocessor will then set the interrupt mask flag high so that no further interrupts may occur. At the end of this cycle, the program counter low will be loaded from address FFFE, and program counter high from location FFFF, therefore transferring program control to the memory vector located at these addresses. The RDY signal must be in the high state for any interrupt to be recognized. A 3KΩ external resistor should be used for proper wire-OR operation.

Non-Maskable Interrupt ($\overline{NMI}$)

A negative going transition on this input requests that a non-maskable interrupt sequence be generated within the microprocessor.

$\overline{NMI}$ is an unconditional interrupt. Following completion of the current instruction, the sequence of operations defined for $\overline{IRQ}$ will be performed, regardless of the state interrupt mask flag. The vestor address loaded into the program counter, low and high, are locations FFFA and FFFB respectively, thereby transferring program control to the memory vector located at these addresses. The instructions loaded at these locations cause the microprocessor to branch to a non-maskable interrupt routine in memory.

$\overline{NMI}$ also requires an external 3KΩ resistor to V_{CC} for proper wire-OR operations.

Inputs $\overline{IRQ}$ and $\overline{NMI}$ are hardware interrupts lines that are sampled during $\emptyset_2$ (phase 2) and will begin the appropriate interrupt routine on the $\emptyset_1$ (phase 1) following the completion of the current instruction.

Set Overflow Flag (S.O.)

A NEGATIVE going edge on this input sets the overflow bit in the Status Code Register. This signal is sampled on the trailing edge of $\emptyset_1$.

SYNC

This output line is provided to identify those cycles in which the microprocessor is doing an OP CODE fetch. The SYNC line goes high during $\emptyset_1$ of an OP CODE fetch and stays high for the remainder of that cycle. If the RDY line is pulled low during the $\emptyset_1$ clock pulse in which SYNC went high, the processor will stop in its current state and will remain in the state until the RDY line goes high. In this manner, the SYNC signal can be used to control RDY to cause single instruction execution.

Reset ($\overline{RES}$)

This input is used to reset or start the microprocessor from a power down condition. During the time that this line is held low, writing to or from the microprocessor is inhibited. When a positive edge is detected on the input, the microprocessor will immediately begin the reset sequence.

After a system initialization time of six clock cycles, the mask interrupt flag will be set and the microprocessor will load the program counter from the memory vector locations FFFC and FFFD. This is the start location for program control.

After V_{CC} reaches 4.75 volts in a power up routine, reset must be held low for at least two clock cycles. At this time the R/W and SYNC signal will become valid.

When the reset signal goes high following these two clock cycles, the microprocessor will proceed with the normal reset procedure detailed above.

Read/Write (R/W)

This output signal is used to control the direction of data transfers between the processor and other circuits on the data bus. A high level on R/W signifies data into the processor; a low is for data transfer out of the processor.

PROGRAMMING CHARACTERISTICS
INSTRUCTION SET — ALPHABETIC SEQUENCE

ADC	Add Memory to Accumulator with Carry	DEC	Decrement Memory by One	PHA	Push Accumulator on Stack
AND	"AND" Memory with Accumulator	DEX	Decrement Index X by One	PHP	Push Processor Status on Stack
ASL	Shift left One Bit (Memory or Accumulator)	DEY	Decrement Index Y by One	PLA	Pull Accumulator from Stack
				PLP	Pull Processor Status from Stack
BCC	Branch on Carry Clear	EOR	"Exclusive-or" Memory with Accumulator		
BCS	Branch on Carry Set			ROL	Rotate One Bit Left (Memory or Accumulator)
BEQ	Branch on Result Zero	INC	Increment Memory by One	ROR	Rotate One Bit Right (Memory or Accumulator)
BIT	Test Bits in Memory with Accumulator	INX	Increment Index X by One	RTI	Return from Interrupt
BMI	Branch on Result Minus	INY	Increment Index Y by One	RTS	Return from Subroutine
BNE	Branch on Result not Zero				
BPL	Branch on Result Plus	JMP	Jump to New Location	SBC	Subtract Memory from Accumulator with Borrow
BRK	Force Break	JSR	Jump to New Location Saving Return Address	SEC	Set Carry Flag
BVC	Branch on Overflow Clear			SED	Set Decimal Mode
BVS	Branch on Overflow Set	LDA	Load Accumulator with Memory	SEI	Set Interrupt Disable Status
		LDX	Load Index X with Memory	STA	Store Accumulator in Memory
CLC	Clear Carry Flag	LDY	Load Index Y with Memory	STX	Store Index X in Memory
CLD	Clear Decimal Mode	LSR	Shift One Bit Right (Memory or Accumulator)	STY	Store Index Y in Memory
CLI	Clear Interrupt Disable Bit				
CLV	Clear Overflow Flag	NOP	No Operation	TAX	Transfer Accumulator to Index X
CMP	Compare Memory and Accumulator			TAY	Transfer Accumulator to Index Y
CPX	Compare Memory and Index X	ORA	"OR" Memory with Accumulator	TSX	Transfer Stack Pointer to Index X
CPY	Compare Memory and Index Y			TXA	Transfer Index X to Accumulator
				TXS	Transfer Index X to Stack Pointer
				TYA	Transfer Index Y to Accumulator

ADDRESSING MODES

Accumulator Addressing

This form of addressing is represented with a one byte instruction, implying an operation on the accumulator.

Immediate Addressing

In immediate addressing, the operand is contained in the second byte of the instruction, with no further memory addressing required.

Absolute Addressing

In absolute addressing, the second byte of the instruction specifies the eight low order bits of the effective address while the third byte specifies the eight high order bits. Thus, the absolute addressing mode allows access to the entire 65K bytes of addressable memory.

Zero Page Addressing

The zero page instructions allow for shorter code and execution times by only fetching the second byte of the instruction and assuming a zero high address byte. Careful use of the zero page can result in significant increase in code efficiency.

Indexed Zero Page Addressing — (X, Y indexing)

This form of addressing is used in conjunction with the index register and is referred to as "Zero Page, X" or "Zero Page, Y." The effective address is calcuated by adding the second byte to the contents of the index register. Since this is a form of "Zero Page" addressing, the content of the second byte references a location in page zero. Additionally due to the "Zero Page" addressing nature of this mode, no carry is added to the high order 8 bits of memory and crossing of page boundaries does not occur.

Indexed Absolute Addressing — (X, Y indexing)

This form of addressing is used in conjunction with X and Y index register and is referred to as "Absolute, X," and "Absolute, Y." The effective address is formed by adding the contents of X or Y to the address contained in the second and third bytes of the instruction. This mode allows the index register to contain the index or count value and the instruction to contain the base address. This type of indexing allows any location referencing and the index to modify multiple fields resulting in reduced coding and execution time.

Implied Addressing

In the implied addressing mode, the address containing the operand is implicitly stated in the operation code of the instruction.

Relative Addressing

Relative addressing is used only with branch instructions and establishes a destination for the conditional branch.

The second byte of the instruction becomes the operand which is an "Offset" added to the contents of the lower eight bits of the program counter when the counter is set at the next instruction. The range of the offset is -128 to $+127$ bytes from the next instruction.

Indexed Indirect Addressing

In indexed indirect addressing (referred to as (Indirect,X)), the second byte of the instruction is added to the contents of the X index register, discarding the carry. The result of this addition points to a memory location on page zero whose contents is the low order eight bits of the effective address. The next memory location in page zero contains the high order eight bits of the effective address. Both memory locations specifying the high and low order bytes of the effective address must be in page zero.

Indirect Indexed Addressing

In indirect indexed addressing (referred to as (Indirect),Y), the second byte of the instruction points to a memory location in page zero. The contents of this memory location is added to the contents of the Y index register, the result being the low order eight bits of the effective address. The carry from this addition is added to the contents of the next page zero memory location, the result being the high order eight bits of the effective address.

Absolute Indirect

The second byte of the instruction contains the low order eight bits of a memory location. The high order eight bits of that memory location is contained in the third byte of the instruction. The contents of the fully specified memory location is the low order byte of the effective address. The next memory location contains the high order byte of the effective address which is loaded into the sixteen bits of the program counter.

Figure 2–3 SY6500 microprocessor architecture and instructions. (Reprinted with permission of Synertek, Inc., all rights reserved.)

interface with the internal 8-bit data bus. PCL represents the lower 8 bits, and PCH represents the upper 8 bits of the program counter register. When the program counter is incremented, it functions as a 16-bit counter; when it loads from the data bus, it functions as two 8-bit registers.

The accumulator register (A) receives data from the internal data bus and provides one of the two data inputs required by the ALU function. The arithmetic and logic unit (ALU) represents the data processing heart of the processor. All of the other architectural features of the CPU may be viewed as mechanisms aimed at efficiently getting data to and from the ALU function.

Index registers are an additional feature that provide a mechanism for greatly reducing the effort of program coding in many cases by simplifying the addressing of portions of a program. Indexed addressing embodies two fundamental characteristics: formation of an address by adding the index number to a base address, and formation of an address by incrementing or decrementing the index number. In program use the base address is provided as part of the instruction that the processor reads from the memory. Thus the processor reads in the base address as secondary parts of a multibyte instruction. The base address is arithmetically added to a copy of the number in the index register, and the resultant sum is then used as an address for another read (or a write) operation. The capability to increment or decrement the index number by one unit then provides the ability to write a simple program loop that reads (or writes) from adjacent locations within a block of memory. Finally, the ability to test the value of the index number provides a convenient way to terminate the program loop after a given number of iterations. Some processors have the capability of incrementing or decrementing the index register by an arbitrary value: the 6500 series microprocessors increments and decrements the index value by one only. As seen in Figure 2-3, the 6500 series microprocessors have two independent 8-bit index registers, X and Y. These registers are not essential to the processor function and could be programmed as a software function, using memory. The availability of the X and Y index registers reduces the amount of programming required and increases the speed of indexed program operation.

The *stack pointer register* (S) represents another added hardware feature that aids processor programming. Somewhat like the index register, the S register generates a sequential list of addresses; however, unlike the index registers in the 6500 series processors the S base address is always a constant equal to hexadecimal 8 (binary 1000). The programmer sets the stack pointer by loading it with an 8-bit number.

When the microprocessor writes data into memory using the S register address (plus 8), the S register is automatically decremented after each write operation, leaving it "pointing" to the next open memory address within the S register field. Every time the microprocessor reads data from the memory using the S register address, the address that is used is one plus the S register value (+8). Thus, the stack pointer read operation automatically reads the last data that were loaded by the S register. The S register address technique therefore implements a "last-in first-out" (LIFO) system. This technique is invaluable in the processing of subroutines, strings of code that are intermittently accessed. Thus just before a subroutine is initiated, the value of the program counter is stored using the S register address. When the subroutine of arbitrary length is completed, the S register is used to retrieve the value of the program counter, which is then loaded into the program counter register. The value of the stack pointer can be particularly appreciated when a first subroutine utilizes a second subroutine, storing a second program counter value before the first PC value has been retrieved. The S register function therefore permits the *nesting* of many subroutines. Nested subroutine programming requirements are often encountered where the processor system utilizes *interrupt* functions, functions that require the interruption of the processing of a first program to process a second (or third) program of higher priority, possibly a program containing transient data (such as from a keyboard) that will be available to the system for only a limited period of time. The stack pointer operations are like index read or write operations except that indexing is done automatically when using the S register but requires an extra instruction when using the index register.

The processor *status register* P is an 8-bit register whose individual bits are used as markers or flags to record certain temporary conditions within the microprocessor. The conditions marked are shown in Figure 2-4. The register is used in conjunction with conditional branch (jump) program steps. That is, a program step may call for a branch only if a particular bit of the P register is in a particular state. Thus the program might branch if, for example, there had been a CARRY.

The CARRY bit of the status register operates in three modes. For programmed arithmetic operations the C bit records whether the last arithmetic operation resulted in a carry (or a borrow). The C bit is also used in register shift operations. The microprocessor can only shift one position for each shift program instruction. All shifting is done either into or out of the C bit; in this mode of operation the C bit also provides a mechanism for serially moving bits from register to register. In the third mode of operation the program can set the C bit either to a 0 or 1.

The Z bit of the status register marks the occurrence of a zero result,

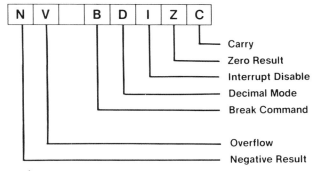

Figure 2–4   6500 microprocessor status register.

which may arise from an arithmetic operation, a load, a register decrement, or a logical operation (AND, or exclusive OR). Again, the value of the P register is that it provides temporary storage of certain selected conditions, conditions that generally are used as part of a conditional branch operation.

The interrupt disable I is a control bit used, as its name implies, to disable the effects of the interrupt request pin. This bit is set and reset under program control.

The D bit controls the arithmetic mode of the processor. In its ONE state all addition and subtraction operations are directed to be decimal arithmetic operations. In its ZERO state the arithmetic operations are performed as simple binary operations.

The BREAK command flag is set automatically by the microprocessor. It is used during interrupt service to determine whether the interrupt was caused by a real interrupt or by a break command. The break command is used during program debugging to break out of a program at a predetermined point to branch to a section where break programming is located.

There is one unused bit within the P register, located between the break and overflow flags.

The V bit provides the overflow flag. When signed binary numbers are being used, the V bit provides the means for knowing that a CARRY bit flowed over into the sign bit area. This bit is the overflow bit during add and subtract instructions, and in the ONE state indicates an overflow into the sign position.

The negative flag N mirrors the sign bit and records the sign after each arithmetic operation. However, since the sign bit is bit 7, the N flag also provides a convenient means for the program to test the most significant bit of the data word that was last moved.

MICROPROCESSOR EXAMPLE—8080

Figure 2-5 shows the architecture of the 8080 microprocessor, which is similar to the architecture of the 6500 series microprocessors. The architectural differences are in detail rather than in principle. The major features of the two microprocessors are very similar; both have the usual ALU, accumulator, instruction decoding, and 16-bit program counter functions. Both architectures employ a 16-bit address bus and an 8-bit data bus.

The architectures differ in the treatment of the internal registers and in the handling of decimal data. The 8080 microprocessor utilizes a small internal memory function to implement its array of five internal registers.* This memory array is built 16 bits wide, so that each of the 5 registers is 16 bits wide as well. This organization permits the 16-bit-wide program counter to be included as one of the five registers. The register array contains the program counter, the stack pointer register, and three general-purpose registers which, under program control, may be used as six 8-bit registers. These general-purpose registers correspond to the two 8-bit index registers of the 6500. Because index registers in the 8080 can be 16 bits wide, indexed memory operations can more conveniently cover larger blocks of memory. The 16-bit-wide registers also add some programming convenience to the system when data words that are more than 8 bits wide are manipulated. However, since the internal data bus and the ALU are only 8 bits wide, data transfers and arithmetic operations must still be done using 8-bit bytes.

Decimal data are treated differently in the 6500 and 8080 processors. The 8080 has a decimal adjust accumulator instruction which automatically converts the 8-bit number in the accumulator into two 4-bit BCDs, plus any carry as required. The 6500 processor directly manipulates BCD data, but must use a programmed routine to convert simple binary numbers to BCD format.

FURTHER MICROPROCESSOR DATA

The appendix to this chapter contains extracts from the manufacturer's data sheets for the widely used 8080A and Z80 single-chip microprocessors. These sheets contain details of the architecture, instruction

---

*The temporary register seen in 8080 literature is not included here since it is not program addressable.

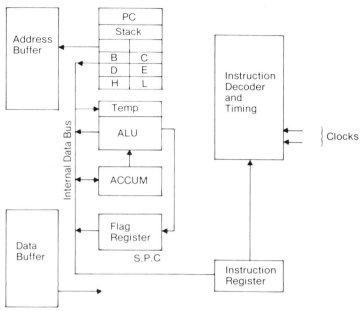

Figure 2–5   8080 microprocessor architecture.

codes and other useful application information. Additional information can be obtained from the manufacturers, of which there are several for each device.

MICROPROCESSOR COMPARISON

Frequently a decision must be made as to what is the "best" microprocessor for a particular purpose. Of course there is no single answer for all purposes, since each device has individual features and costs that make it more applicable for one job or another. The question of word size and addressing ability has already been discussed. Often the speed of execution is cited as an important feature, but here the clock frequency, which determines the speed of elementary microinstructions, is not a reliable guide, since the number of microcycles to accomplish a given task such as memory fetch differs from microprocessor to microprocessor. Speed is not the only criterion; others include the versatility of the instruction set and the ability to use memory efficiently.

The most reliable way to evaluate a microprocessor is to try it out on your particular job. If time and funds to accomplish this are lacking, a series of "benchmarks" can serve as a reliable guide. Benchmarks are elementary tasks chosen to test the ability of microprocessors (or any other computer) in competition with one another with respect to execution time and other qualities such as memory utilization. Table 2-1 summarizes the results of such a benchmark comparison conducted on a number of microprocessors by Allan Flippin and published in *Microcomputing* magazine. The table reports the performance of four common 8-bit microprocessors and one 16-bit, the LSI-11. In addition to the 8-bit devices discussed in this chapter the table includes the Z-80 and the 6800. The clock speed chosen was 2 microseconds for the 6502 and 6800 and 4 microseconds for the 8080 and Z-80. The 16-bit LSI-11 uses a 350-nanosecond clock, and in addition has special features such as extended arithmetic hardware and general-purpose registers.

There are four separate benchmarks, each a separate task. *Table lookup* refers to two tables, each with corresponding entries as if it were a conversion table (e.g., feet to meters). The first table is searched for a value; if found, the corresponding entry in the second table is referenced. If not found, this condition is reported as an error. *Block move* refers to the transfer of a number of ASCII characters from one location (source field) to another (destination field). An analogous task would be the transfer of a buffer memory containing a line of typed characters from a keyboard (1 to 255 characters) and terminated by a carriage return, to a place in main memory. *Jump table* refers to a jump move to an entry in a table stored in memory; the address of the entry is determined randomly by another memory location. Arithmetic processing is represented by a *multiply* operation, consisting of a double-word unsigned numbers representing multiplicand and multiplier.

The qualities measured by these benchmark tests include ease of programming, memory utilization, and execution time in microseconds. Ease of programming is measured in terms of the number of instructions required, although no doubt other individual factors should be considered. The memory utilized is specified in bytes (8 bits).

The results show no clear superiority in all features, even for the "professional" LSI-11. Although its 16-bit capability and architecture give it the best rating overall in memory and programming ease, it is beaten in terms of speed by each of the 8-bit devices except the 8080. In terms of speed the 6502 was judged best; the Z-80 used the least instructions.

Tests like these are not unequivocable, but may suggest where to look for solutions to particular problems. The original article is recommended, not only for coverage of other microprocessors but also to suggest to the reader how these tests can be set up for your own problems.

Table 2-1 Microprocessor Benchmark Comparisons

Micro-processor	Table Lookup			Block Move			Jump Table			Multiply		
	Instruc-tions	Memory (bytes)	Execu-tion Time (μs)	Instruc-tions	Memory (bytes)	Execu-tion Time (μs)	Instruc-tions	Memory (bytes)	Execu-tion Time (μs)	Instruc-tions	Memory (bytes)	Execu-tion Time (μs)
Z-80	9	18	98	11	22	1200	11	13	15	15	26	93
6502	9	21	81	16	31	1169	8	18	14	17	32	85
6800	12	25	99	16	29	1430	9	18	16	14	26	87
8080	12	24	107	14	23	1233	11	13	16	19	31	130
LSI-11	8	26	159	11	30	1876	3	10	19	2	8	37

Source: *Microcomputing*, 26–35 (March 1980).

APPENDIX: MICROPROCESSOR ARCHITECTURE

8080A ARCHITECTURE AND INSTRUCTION SET*

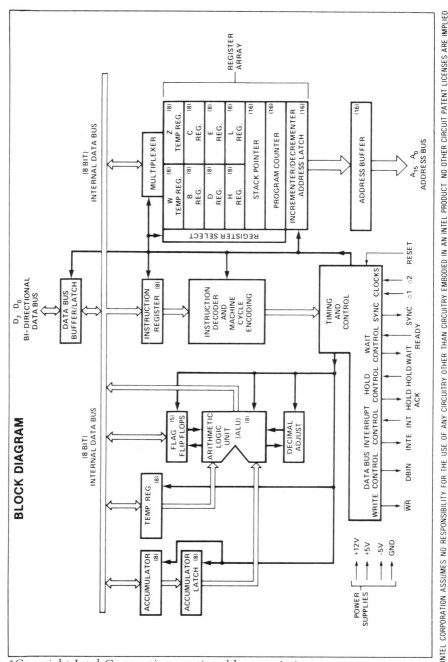

BLOCK DIAGRAM

*Copyright Intel Corporation, reprinted by permission.

8080 INSTRUCTION SET
Summary of Processor Instructions

Mnemonic	Description	D7	D6	D5	D4	D3	D2	D1	D0	Clock[2] Cycles
MOVE, LOAD, AND STORE										
MOV r1,r2	Move register to register	0	1	D	D	D	S	S	S	5
MOV M,r	Move register to memory	0	1	1	1	0	S	S	S	7
MOV r,M	Move memory to register	0	1	D	D	D	1	1	0	7
MVI r	Move immediate register	0	0	D	D	D	1	1	0	7
MVI M	Move immediate memory	0	0	1	1	0	1	1	0	10
LXI B	Load immediate register Pair B & C	0	0	0	0	0	0	0	1	10
LXI D	Load immediate register Pair D & E	0	0	0	1	0	0	0	1	10
LXI H	Load immediate register Pair H & L	0	0	1	0	0	0	0	1	10
STAX B	Store A indirect	0	0	0	0	0	0	1	0	7
STAX D	Store A indirect	0	0	0	1	0	0	1	0	7
LDAX B	Load A indirect	0	0	0	0	1	0	1	0	7
LDAX D	Load A indirect	0	0	0	1	1	0	1	0	7
STA	Store A direct	0	0	1	1	0	0	1	0	13
LDA	Load A direct	0	0	1	1	1	0	1	0	13
SHLD	Store H & L direct	0	0	1	0	0	0	1	0	16
LHLD	Load H & L direct	0	0	1	0	1	0	1	0	16
XCHG	Exchange D & E H & L Registers	1	1	1	0	1	0	1	1	4
STACK OPS										
PUSH B	Push register Pair B & C on stack	1	1	0	0	0	1	0	1	11
PUSH D	Push register Pair D & E on stack	1	1	0	1	0	1	0	1	11
PUSH H	Push register Pair H & L on stack	1	1	1	0	0	1	0	1	11
PUSH PSW	Push A and Flags on stack	1	1	1	1	0	1	0	1	11
POP B	Pop register Pair B & C off stack	1	1	0	0	0	0	0	1	10
POP D	Pop register Pair D & E off stack	1	1	0	1	0	0	0	1	10
POP H	Pop register Pair H & L off stack	1	1	1	0	0	0	0	1	10
POP PSW	Pop A and Flags off stack	1	1	1	1	0	0	0	1	10
XTHL	Exchange top of stack H & L	1	1	1	0	0	0	1	1	18
SPHL	H & L to stack pointer	1	1	1	1	1	0	0	1	5
LXI SP	Load immediate stack pointer	0	0	1	1	0	0	0	1	10
INX SP	Increment stack pointer	0	0	1	1	0	0	1	1	5
DCX SP	Decrement stack pointer	0	0	1	1	1	0	1	1	5
JUMP										
JMP	Jump unconditional	1	1	0	0	0	0	1	1	10
JC	Jump on carry	1	1	0	1	1	0	1	0	10
JNC	Jump on no carry	1	1	0	1	0	0	1	0	10
JZ	Jump on zero	1	1	0	0	1	0	1	0	10
JNZ	Jump on no zero	1	1	0	0	0	0	1	0	10
JP	Jump on positive	1	1	1	1	0	0	1	0	10
JM	Jump on minus	1	1	1	1	1	0	1	0	10
JPE	Jump on parity even	1	1	1	0	1	0	1	0	10

Mnemonic	Description	D7	D6	D5	D4	D3	D2	D1	D0	Clock[2] Cycles
JPO	Jump on parity odd	1	1	1	0	0	0	1	0	10
PCHL	H & L to program counter	1	1	1	0	1	0	0	1	5
CALL										
CALL	Call unconditional	1	1	0	0	1	1	0	1	17
CC	Call on carry	1	1	0	1	1	1	0	0	11/17
CNC	Call on no carry	1	1	0	1	0	1	0	0	11/17
CZ	Call on zero	1	1	0	0	1	1	0	0	11/17
CNZ	Call on no zero	1	1	0	0	0	1	0	0	11/17
CP	Call on positive	1	1	1	1	0	1	0	0	11/17
CM	Call on minus	1	1	1	1	1	1	0	0	11/17
CPE	Call on parity even	1	1	1	0	1	1	0	0	11/17
CPO	Call on parity odd	1	1	1	0	0	1	0	0	11/17
RETURN										
RET	Return	1	1	0	0	1	0	0	1	10
RC	Return on carry	1	1	0	1	1	0	0	0	5/11
RNC	Return on no carry	1	1	0	1	0	0	0	0	5/11
RZ	Return on zero	1	1	0	0	1	0	0	0	5/11
RNZ	Return on no zero	1	1	0	0	0	0	0	0	5/11
RP	Return on positive	1	1	1	1	0	0	0	0	5/11
RM	Return on minus	1	1	1	1	1	0	0	0	5/11
RPE	Return on parity even	1	1	1	0	1	0	0	0	5/11
RPO	Return on parity odd	1	1	1	0	0	0	0	0	5/11
RESTART										
RST	Restart	1	1	A	A	A	1	1	1	11
INCREMENT AND DECREMENT										
INR r	Increment register	0	0	D	D	D	1	0	0	5
DCR r	Decrement register	0	0	D	D	D	1	0	1	5
INR M	Increment memory	0	0	1	1	0	1	0	0	10
DCR M	Decrement memory	0	0	1	1	0	1	0	1	10
INX B	Increment B & C registers	0	0	0	0	0	0	1	1	5
INX D	Increment D & E registers	0	0	0	1	0	0	1	1	5
INX H	Increment H & L registers	0	0	1	0	0	0	1	1	5
DCX B	Decrement B & C	0	0	0	0	1	0	1	1	5
DCX D	Decrement D & E	0	0	0	1	1	0	1	1	5
DCX H	Decrement H & L	0	0	1	0	1	0	1	1	5
ADD										
ADD r	Add register to A	1	0	0	0	0	S	S	S	4
ADC r	Add register to A with carry	1	0	0	0	1	S	S	S	4
ADD M	Add memory to A	1	0	0	0	0	1	1	0	7
ADC M	Add memory to A with carry	1	0	0	0	1	1	1	0	7
ADI	Add immediate to A	1	1	0	0	0	1	1	0	7
ACI	Add immediate to A with carry	1	1	0	0	1	1	1	0	7
DAD B	Add B & C to H & L	0	0	0	0	1	0	0	1	10
DAD D	Add D & E to H & L	0	0	0	1	1	0	0	1	10
DAD H	Add H & L to H & L	0	0	1	0	1	0	0	1	10
DAD SP	Add stack pointer to H & L	0	0	1	1	1	0	0	1	10

NOTES 1 DDD or SSS B 000 C 001 D 010 E 011 H 100 L 101 Memory 110 A 111
2 Two possible cycle times (6/12) indicate instruction cycles dependent on condition flags

*All mnemonics copyright
©Intel Corporation 1977

MCS-80/85

8080A/8080A-1/8080A-2

Summary of Processor Instructions (Cont.)

Mnemonic	Description	D_7	D_6	D_5	D_4	D_3	D_2	D_1	D_0	Clock[2] Cycles
SUBTRACT										
SUB r	Subtract register from A	1	0	0	1	0	S	S	S	4
SBB r	Subtract register from A with borrow	1	0	0	1	1	S	S	S	4
SUB M	Subtract memory from A	1	0	0	1	0	1	1	0	7
SBB M	Subtract memory from A with borrow	1	0	0	1	1	1	1	0	7
SUI	Subtract immediate from A	1	1	0	1	0	1	1	0	7
SBI	Subtract immediate from A with borrow	1	1	0	1	1	1	1	0	7
LOGICAL										
ANA r	And register with A	1	0	1	0	0	S	S	S	4
XRA r	Exclusive Or register with A	1	0	1	0	1	S	S	S	4
ORA r	Or register with A	1	0	1	1	0	S	S	S	4
CMP r	Compare register with A	1	0	1	1	1	S	S	S	4
ANA M	And memory with A	1	0	1	0	0	1	1	0	7
XRA M	Exclusive Or memory with A	1	0	1	0	1	1	1	0	7
ORA M	Or memory with A	1	0	1	1	0	1	1	0	7
CMP M	Compare memory with A	1	0	1	1	1	1	1	0	7
ANI	And immediate with A	1	1	1	0	0	1	1	0	7
XRI	Exclusive Or immediate with A	1	1	1	0	1	1	1	0	7
ORI	Or immediate with A	1	1	1	1	0	1	1	0	7
CPI	Compare immediate with A	1	1	1	1	1	1	1	0	7
ROTATE										
RLC	Rotate A left	0	0	0	0	0	1	1	1	4
RRC	Rotate A right	0	0	0	0	1	1	1	1	4
RAL	Rotate A left through carry	0	0	0	1	0	1	1	1	4
RAR	Rotate A right through carry	0	0	0	1	1	1	1	1	4
SPECIALS										
CMA	Complement A	0	0	1	0	1	1	1	1	4
STC	Set carry	0	0	1	1	0	1	1	1	4
CMC	Complement carry	0	0	1	1	1	1	1	1	4
DAA	Decimal adjust A	0	0	1	0	0	1	1	1	4
INPUT/OUTPUT										
IN	Input	1	1	0	1	1	0	1	1	10
OUT	Output	1	1	0	1	0	0	1	1	10
CONTROL										
EI	Enable Interrupts	1	1	1	1	1	0	1	1	4
DI	Disable Interrupt	1	1	1	1	0	0	1	1	4
NOP	No-operation	0	0	0	0	0	0	0	0	4
HLT	Halt	0	1	1	1	0	1	1	0	7

NOTES 1 DDD or SSS B=000 C=001 D=010 E=011 H=100 L=101 Memory=110 A=111
      2 Two possible cycle times (6/12) indicate instruction cycles dependent on condition flags

Z-80 ARCHITECTURE†

A block diagram of the internal architecture of the Z80-CPU is shown in Figure 2.0-1 The diagram shows all of the major elements in the CPU and it should be referred to throughout the following description.

Z80-CPU BLOCK DIAGRAM

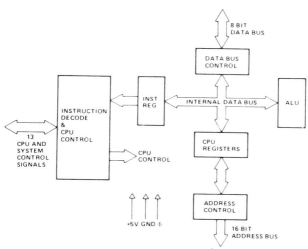

2.1 CPU REGISTERS

The Z80-CPU contains 208 bits of R/W memory that are accessible to the programmer. Figure 2.0-2 illustrates how this memory is configured into eighteen 8-bit registers and four 16-bit registers. All Z80 registers are implemented using static RAM. The registers include two sets of six general purpose registers that may be used individually as 8-bit registers or in pairs as 16-bit registers. There are also two sets of accumulator and flag registers.

Special Purpose Registers

1. **Program Counter (PC).** The program counter holds the 16-bit address of the current instruction being fetched from memory. The PC is automatically incremented after its contents have been transferred to the address lines. When a program jump occurs the new value is automatically placed in the PC, overriding the incrementer.

2. **Stack Pointer (SP).** The stack pointer holds the 16-bit address of the current top of a stack located anywhere in external system RAM memory. The external stack memory is organized as a last-in first-out (LIFO) file. Data can be pushed onto the stack from specific CPU registers or popped off of the stack into specific CPU registers through the execution of PUSH and POP instructions. The data popped from the stack is always the last data pushed onto it. The stack allows simple implementation of multiple level interrupts, unlimited subroutine nesting and simplification of many types of data manipulation.

†Copyright Mostek 1978, reprinted by permission (specifications subject to change).

Z80-CPU REGISTER CONFIGURATION

	MAIN REG SET		ALTERNATE REG SET	
	ACCUMULATOR A	FLAGS F	ACCUMULATOR A'	FLAGS F
	B	C	B'	C'
	D	E	D'	E'
	H	L	H'	L'

GENERAL PURPOSE REGISTERS

INTERRUPT VECTOR I	MEMORY REFRESH R
INDEX REGISTER IX	
INDEX REGISTER IY	
STACK POINTER SP	
PROGRAM COUNTER PC	

SPECIAL PURPOSE REGISTERS

3. **Two Index Registers (IX & IY).** The two independent index registers hold a 16-bit base address that is used in indexed addressing modes. In this mode, an index register is used as a base to point to a region in memory from which data is to be stored or retrieved. An additional byte is included in indexed instructions to specify a displacement from this base. This displacement is specified as a two's complement signed integer. This mode of addressing greatly simplifies many types of programs, especially where tables of data are used.

4. **Interrupt Page Address Register (I).** The Z80-CPU can be operated in a mode where an indirect call to any memory location can be achieved in response to an interrupt. The I Register is used for this purpose to store the high order 8-bits of the indirect address while the interrupting device provides the lower 8-bits of the address. This feature allows interrupt routines to be dynamically located anywhere in memory with absolute minimal access time to the routine.

5. **Memory Refresh Register (R).** The Z80-CPU contains a memory refresh counter to enable dynamic memories to be used with the same ease as static memories. This 7-bit register is automatically incremented after each instruction fetch. The data in the refresh counter is sent out on the lower portion of the address bus along with a refresh control signal while the CPU is decoding and executing the fetched instruction. This mode of refresh is totally transparent to the programmer and does not slow down the CPU operation. The programmer can load the R register for testing purposes, but this register is normally not used by the programmer.

Accumulator and Flag Registers

The CPU includes two independent 8-bit accumulators and associated 8-bit flag registers. The accumulator holds the results of 8-bit arithmetic or logical operations while the flag register indicates specific conditions for 8 or 16-bit operations, such as indicating whether or not the result of an operation is equal to zero. The programmer selects the accumulator and flag pair that he wishes to work with with a single exchange instruction so that he may easily work with either pair.

General Purpose Registers

There are two matched sets of general purpose registers, each set containing six 8-bit registers that may be used individually as 8-bit registers or as 16-bit register pairs by the programmer. One set is called BC, DE, and HL while the complementary set is called BD', DE' and HL'. At any one time the programmer can select either set of registers to work with through a single exchange command for the entire set. In systems where fast interrupt response is required, one set of general purpose registers and an accumulator/flag register may be reserved for handling this very fast routine. Only a simple exchange command need be executed to go between the routines. This greatly reduces interrupt service time by eliminating the requirement for saving and retrieving register contents in the external stack during interrupt or subroutine processing. These general purpose registers are used for a wide range of applications by the programmer. They also simplify programming, especially in ROM based systems where little external read/write memory is available.

2.2 ARITHMETIC & LOGIC UNIT (ALU)

The 8-bit arithmetic and logical instructions of the CPU are executed in the ALU. Internally the ALU communicates with the registers and the external data bus on the internal data bus. The type of functions performed by the ALU include:

Add	Left or right shifts or rotates (arithmetic and logical)
Subtract	Increment
Logical AND	Decrement
Logical OR	Set bit
Logical Exclusive OR	Reset bit
Compare	Test bit

2.3 INSTRUCTION REGISTER AND CPU CONTROL

As each instruction is fetched from memory, it is placed in the instruction register and decoded. The control section performs this function and then generates and supplies all of the control signals necessary to read or write data from or to the registers, controls the ALU and provides all required external control signals.

3

Signal Pathways

SIGNAL BUSES

From the discussion of Chapters 1 and 2 the reader will perceive that the complicated functions obtained by digital processor–based systems are constructed from simple logic circuit building blocks. These are interconnected by parallel signal pathways called *buses*. In a general way these circuit blocks are controlled by addressing functions that cause the individual circuits to be activated as needed. When the circuit functions are close together, as they are on a microprocessor chip, the addressing and decoding are all done together and the formalism of addressing individual circuits with addresses is obscured. If the circuits are further apart, as they are in a processor system with numerous peripheral devices, the formalism of device addressing becomes more apparent.

Just as the circuit functions are assembled from a few basic logic circuits, so are the signal pathways that interconnect these circuits. We saw in Chapter 2 that the microprocessor is essentially oriented around a *data bus*. The considerations of Chapter 1 indicated that the two primary pathways for the microprocessor system are the address bus and the data bus. This chapter considers the practical problems of using signal buses in real systems. Within the microprocessor system buses exist at several levels of organization. The microprocessor chip discussed in Chapter 2 is always mounted on a circuit board, and this board invariably carries an address bus and a data bus. But these two buses must always leave the processor circuit board (card) for interconnection to other cards, providing expanded functions of memory, peripheral device ports, digital to analog conversion, and other special functions such as audio output. The imperfections of practical signal buses become increasingly apparent as they become longer. These imperfections make it necessary to provide an additional level of signal control that operates in parallel with the two major buses. This *control bus* carries *strobing* and *clock* signals and generally *interrupt request* (IR) signals also. The purpose of these signals is made clearer in this chapter.

BUS SIGNALS

An individual signal line of a bus may be thought of as a resistive-capacitive (R-C) circuit driven by a switched voltage source, as seen in Figure 3-1.

In this representation the digital driving signal switches between a high and a low voltage representing the change between a ONE and ZERO state. The line driver can only deliver a limited amount of current to the load RL; this limitation is effectively represented by the charge and discharge resistances R_3 and R_2, respectively.

Inductance in the bus line, represented by the inductance L, may be a further imperfection in the bus circuit. However, for short bus lines this inductance can generally be neglected. There is always shunt capacity, represented by C in Figure 3-1. This capacity is produced by the distributed capacitance of the line, the driver capacitance, and the capacitance associated with the load itself. In most systems the load capacitance provides the greater portion of the total, although the distributed capacity of the line can become very large as the line length increases.

The main point of the schematic representation of Figure 3-1 is that there is an *electrical time constant* for the circuit which limits the rate at which the received signal E_0 can change in response to a change in the switch S. That is, even if the switch S changes its position in zero time, there is an inevitable delay before that change in state can be sensed at the load. If all inductance in the bus line is neglected, the relation between input and output signals is as illustrated in Figure 3-2.

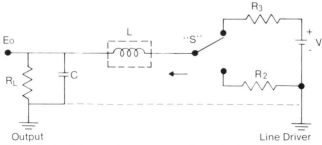

Figure 3–1   Schematic representation of a bus signal line.

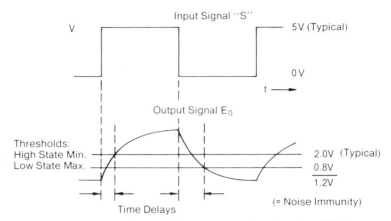

Figure 3–2 Waveforms of Figure 3–1 showing signal delay.

As shown in the figure, the digital input information, as received, is degraded from its original sharp square-wave shape. The form of the received transitions is exponential. The rising waveform is represented mathematically as $V(1 - e^{-t/R_cC})$, and the falling waveform as Ve^{-t/R_3C}. It can be shown by plotting these expressions that the RC products, which are the time constants of the circuit, are the crucial values in determining how much delay the circuit exhibits in reaching the change of state threshold. Reducing either the resistance or the capacitance reduces the time constant, increases the slope of the received waveform, and correspondingly speeds up the circuit by reducing the time to reach the threshold. The actual delay associated with the bus circuit depends on the RC time constant, the digital switching, voltage (V), and the threshold itself, which depends on the switching characteristics associated with the circuit receiving the signal.

In a multiwire parallel bus, the parameters that determine delay are not necessarily identical for each wire; consequently, the receiving circuits do not all change state at the same speed and at the same time. A decoder, operating on data received from the parallel bus produces many different decoded results during the time of data transition. This situation, unless explicitly corrected, will cause chaos within the system where, in general, many decoders are all connected to the same address bus in transition. The problems associated with the uncertainty in bus data during times of data transition are avoided, rather than eliminated, through the simple strategy of waiting a suitable time following the occurrence of a data transition, until all the data lines of the bus have had sufficient time to settle to their correct HIGH or LOW stages.

Generally, a compromise must be reached between slowing down the data transmission rate and assuring the availability of reliable data. Most system designs resolve the problem of data integrity by providing an enabling pulse that is delayed relative to the time of initiation of data transitions. This signal is called a *strobe pulse.* By design the data have had time to settle to a stable state when it is strobed. A strobe pulse is usually associated with a particular class of data such as an address bus, a data bus, or I/0 data. By this association with a particular type of data, the minimum delay needed to accommodate the worst case delay can more readily be predicted and the strobe signal set to provide the optimum delay.

Clock signals, another type of strobe signal used in digital systems, are usually the highest frequency periodic signal found in the system and form the basis of all system timing. By contrast the ordinary variety of strobe signal is a relatively low frequency signal and is often aperiodic. The most common use of clock pulses is by devices that are *edge sensitive,* meaning that they change state immediately following the occurrence of a particular transition edge (e.g., HIGH to LOW) of the clock signal. Figure 3-3 provides an example of a 4-bit counter integrated circuit timing diagram which illustrates the change in state of the four output signals, Q_A, Q_B, Q_C, and Q_D, immediately following the LOW to HIGH transition of the clock signal. By arranging for the storage type circuits of the system to change state only at the time of the trailing edge of the clock pulse, a known time interval is established during which the circuit state transition must be completed. Typically, a rising, trailing edge-triggered circuit requires that the input signals to the circuit be quiescent during the low portion of the clock pulse. Thus in the fastest, most demanding situation, where the clock signal is a square wave, the circuit logic has a required settling time of 50% of the clock period. In slower, less demanding situations the asymmetric negative clock pulse can be kept at a minimum width, and the circuit logic then has almost the entire clock period in which to settle to its next state.

Both the strobe and clock signals are used in conjunction with other data signals. By acting as enabling signals, they effectively synchronize the time of transition of received data. They provide a precisely defined time within which all data must settle, and also force the associated circuits to remain inactive until the data reach their stable and reliable state.

Associated with all random access memories is a READ-WRITE (R/W) control line, which is usually also used as a write strobe signal. This signal controls whether the memory block will enter data from the

SN54160, SN54162, SN74160, SN74162 SYNCHRONOUS DECADE COUNTERS

typical clear, preset, count, and inhibit sequences

Illustrated below is the following sequence:
1. Clear outputs to zero.
2. Preset to BCD seven.
3. Count to eight, nine, zero, one, two, and three.
4. Inhibit

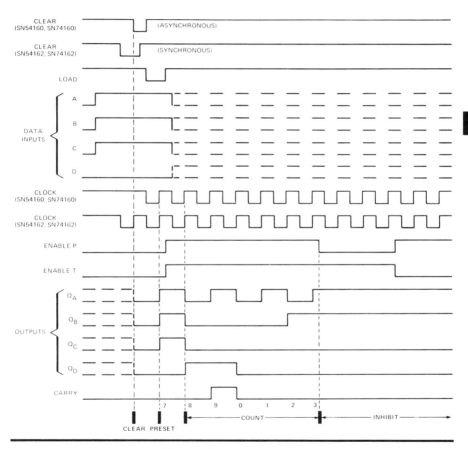

TEXAS INSTRUMENTS
INCORPORATED
POST OFFICE BOX 5012 • DALLAS, TEXAS 75222

Figure 3–3   Waveforms of a 4-bit counter. (Reprinted by permission of Texas Instruments, Inc.)

62

data bus into the memory, or whether it will be in the READ state, passively supplying data from within the memory. Obviously, great care must be exercised to ensure memory integrity and to avoid spurious writing into the memory. Accordingly, the R/W control normally rests in its READ state, and the control is pulsed only when a write operation is to be performed. The WRITE control pulse thus effectively serves as a WRITE strobe pulse, and is timed to ensure that correct data are available at the memory at the time of memory change (writing).

Reading is usually from the memory to the processor. After the processor provides the required address, the read data is entered into the processor from the data bus. The processor also must strobe in the data, but this strobe may be internal to the processor and not visible outside the microprocessor chip.

As discussed in Chapter 1, each entity that communicates with the processor is addressed by the processor, and the actual selection of the device is accomplished by the decoding of the selection address. The physical process of decoding may be done either at the processor location or remotely, at the site of the peripheral device. Generally, when the system contains only a few peripheral devices, it is most efficient to locate the device decoder with the processor, for then a single integrated circuit decoder can accomplish all the required device decoding and the 16-wire address bus need not be connected to all the peripheral devices since a single select line will do.

If the device slection decoder is strobed, its decoded output selection signals are both selection and strobe signal combined, and the circuits receiving these signals can use them directly as both selection and enabling signals. Figure 3-4 provides data on a type 74154 integrated circuit decoder. In this circuit 4 address lines (A, B, C, D) decode into 16 decoded signals $(Q_0, Q_1, \ldots, Q_{15})$, and $G1$ and $G2$ are disabling signal paths; a HIGH level on either input disables the decoder function. When both go LOW together, they function as a strobing input.

Interrupt signals represent a special kind of bus control in that they effectively control all the buses by forcing the processor to execute predetermined functions. An interrupt operation is used to service an input device that requires immediate attention but at a relatively infrequent rate. A keyboard provides an example of this kind of input device. The use of an interrupt function avoids the need to *poll*, or query, repetitively at high speed, a device that provides data at a low rate. An interrupt operation causes the processor to jump automatically to a special interrupt program. Immediately before this jump is made, the processor automatically stores the contents of its status register and program counter (see Chapter 2). At the completion of the interrupt logic

FUNCTION TABLE

INPUTS						OUTPUTS															
G1	G2	D	C	B	A	0	1	2	3	4	5	6	7	8	9	10	11	12	13	14	15
L	L	L	L	L	L	L	H	H	H	H	H	H	H	H	H	H	H	H	H	H	H
L	L	L	L	L	H	H	L	H	H	H	H	H	H	H	H	H	H	H	H	H	H
L	L	L	L	H	L	H	H	L	H	H	H	H	H	H	H	H	H	H	H	H	H
L	L	L	L	H	H	H	H	H	L	H	H	H	H	H	H	H	H	H	H	H	H
L	L	L	H	L	L	H	H	H	H	L	H	H	H	H	H	H	H	H	H	H	H
L	L	L	H	L	H	H	H	H	H	H	L	H	H	H	H	H	H	H	H	H	H
L	L	L	H	H	L	H	H	H	H	H	H	L	H	H	H	H	H	H	H	H	H
L	L	L	H	H	H	H	H	H	H	H	H	H	L	H	H	H	H	H	H	H	H
L	L	H	L	L	L	H	H	H	H	H	H	H	H	L	H	H	H	H	H	H	H
L	L	H	L	L	H	H	H	H	H	H	H	H	H	H	L	H	H	H	H	H	H
L	L	H	L	H	L	H	H	H	H	H	H	H	H	H	H	L	H	H	H	H	H
L	L	H	L	H	H	H	H	H	H	H	H	H	H	H	H	H	L	H	H	H	H
L	L	H	H	L	L	H	H	H	H	H	H	H	H	H	H	H	H	L	H	H	H
L	L	H	H	L	H	H	H	H	H	H	H	H	H	H	H	H	H	H	L	H	H
L	L	H	H	H	L	H	H	H	H	H	H	H	H	H	H	H	H	H	H	L	H
L	L	H	H	H	H	H	H	H	H	H	H	H	H	H	H	H	H	H	H	H	L
L	H	X	X	X	X	H	H	H	H	H	H	H	H	H	H	H	H	H	H	H	H
H	L	X	X	X	X	H	H	H	H	H	H	H	H	H	H	H	H	H	H	H	H
H	H	X	X	X	X	H	H	H	H	H	H	H	H	H	H	H	H	H	H	H	H

H = high level, L = low level, X = irrelevant

functional block diagram and schematics of inputs and outputs

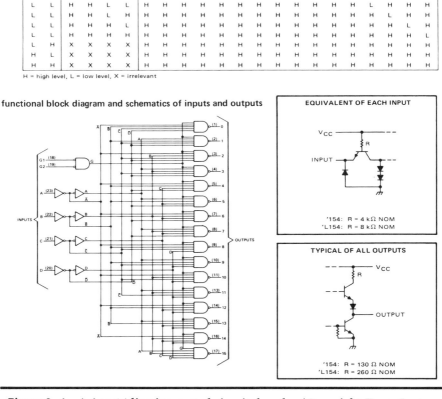

Figure 3–4 A 4 to 16 line integrated circuit decoder. (Copyright Texas Instruments, Inc., reprinted by permission.)

program the processor restores its status and program counter values, then continues processing the original programs. Usually a system has more than one device that can cause an interrupt, and special schemes are devised to handle the cases where the system receives several interrupt requests simultaneously.

BUS DRIVERS

The individual signal wires of a bus are generally characterized as having a high signal load, significant stray capacity, and a small amount of series inductance. Generally, buses longer than 18 inches require special terminating resistors. This terminating resistance is approximately equal to the characteristic impedance of the signal wire, which generally has a low value. The net effect is to require a bus driver circuit that has substantial current drive capability. There are several types of drivers, including the logical-OR, wired-OR, and tristate. The driver and bus type are determined by microprocessor architecture.

The tristate driver circuit represents the best all-purpose driver. It has three output states representing HIGH, LOW, and OFF (or high impedance). The existence of this OFF state makes it very convenient to multiplex or interconnect many circuits on a common bus. When a circuit is in its OFF state, it appears as though it is not in the system; thus many functions can be connected to the same bus line through such drivers. The advantage of the high-impedance OFF state is that the bus itself can then act as a sort of "clothesline," with many tristate buffers strung along it like clothespins on a line. In the absence of a bus driver with a high-impedance state, the signals from each source would have to be conducted to a centrally located multiplexing circuit; by contrast the tristate buffers act as a spatially distributed multiplexer. Figure 3-5 shows a manufacturer's data sheet for a tristate quad bus driver. A final advantage for this type of circuit may be inferred from the schematic diagram. It is seen that the signal output is taken off at a point where two transistors are stacked in series. When not in the OFF state, either the lower transistor is ON while the upper transistor is OFF or vice versa. With either transistor ON the circuit has a low source impedance, which means that the driver can supply a relatively large current to its load. In terms of the representative circuit of Figure 3-1, the resistances R_2 and R_3 are low and the RC time constant for the driver is consequently small, ensuring that the circuit has a fast rise time and correspondingly a minimum delay.

The data presented in Figure 3-5 are typical of the information pro-

DIGITAL 8T SERIES INTERFACE TTL/MSI

DESCRIPTION

The 8T09 is a high speed quad bus driver device for applications requiring up to 25 loads interconnected on a single bus.

The tri-state outputs present a high impedance to the bus when disabled, (control input "1") and active drive when enabled (control input "0"). This eliminates the resistor pull-up requirement while providing performance superior to open collector schemes. Each output can sink 40mA and drive 300pF loading with guaranteed propagation delay less than 20 nanoseconds.

PIN CONFIGURATIONS (Top View)

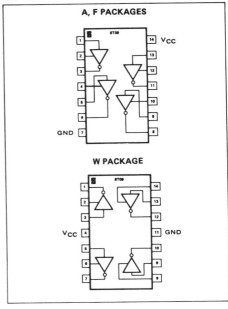

LOGIC DIAGRAM AND TRUTH TABLE

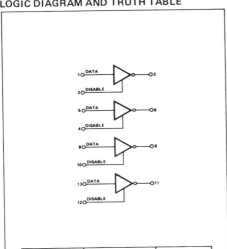

Data	Disable	Output
0	0	1
1	0	0
0	1	Hi- Z
1	1	Hi- Z

V_{CC} = (14)
GND = (7)
( ) = Denotes Pin Numbers for
14 Pin Dual-in-Line Package

SCHEMATIC DIAGRAM

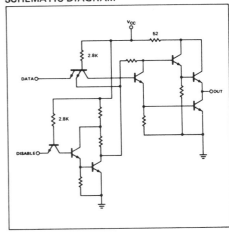

Figure 3–5 Tristate bus driver integrated circuit. (Copyright Signetics Corp., reprinted by permission.)

vided by manufacturers of integrated circuits. The information shows the package, the logic diagram with associated pin-out references, and the schematic diagram. More complicated circuits may have the schematic diagram omitted from the logic diagram. It should be noted that each of the four inverting buffer circuits is provided with a disable control. When this control is driven positive to the ONE state, the buffer is placed in its disabled, high-impedance condition. Correspondingly, when the disable line is driven low to its ZERO state, the circuit is enabled and each of the four individual circuits acts as an inverting buffer amplifier.

Figure 3-6 shows an open-collector circuit, another type of bus driver. As seen in the circuit schematic diagram, the circuit output point is the collector of an *NPN* transistor; there are no components connecting the collector to the positive voltage (VCC) line. The high-impedance state is obtained by driving the circuit input LOW, cutting off the output transistor. Since the buffer circuit has no disable control input, a gating circuit is generally connected to the input to provide the required control. For normal buffer amplifier operation, the bus line must provide a pull-up resistor connected to a positive voltage line. Advantages of this circuit are its low cost and the need for only one pull-up resistor for each bus line, even when a number of open-collector drivers are connected to the line. Disadvantages of this type of driver are the requirement for gating control preceding the driver, the need for driver current to be shared by the pull-up resistor and the line load, and reduced circuit speed, since a practical pull-up resistor provides a relatively large *RC* time constant for positive line signals.

Bus lines longer than about 18 inches have inductive effects, causing positive and negative spike transients that occur at the time of signal state change. These inductive transients are reduced and controlled by loading the lines with resistors. For lines driven by open-collector drivers, the pull-up resistor partially serves this function. If only line transients are considered, the optimum line loading is the characteristic impedance of the line, a value that is typically in the range of 150 ohms. However, a 5-volt signal swing requires that a 33-milliampere current be supplied to the 150-ohm resistive load; a typical bus driver, such as those in Figures 3-5 and 3-6, has a 40-mA current capacity, so a 150 pull-up resistor uses up most of this drive capability. One approach to resolving this problem is the use of two resistors on the bus line, as shown in Figure 3-7. The bus to ground resistor draws less current from the driver, but the pair of resistors presents a 150-ohm impedance by appearing in parallel to the line.

Signetics

HEX INVERTER BUFFER/DRIVER WITH OPEN COLLECTOR HIGH VOLTAGE OUTPUTS

S5406−A,F,W • S5416−A,F,W • N7406−A,F • N7416−A,F

DIGITAL 54/74 TTL SERIES

S5406
S5416
N7406
N7416

DESCRIPTION

The 54/7406 and 54/7416 Hex Inverter Buffer/Drivers features standard TTL inputs with inverted high voltage, high current, open collector outputs for interface with MOS, lamps or relays. The 54/7406 minimum output breakdown is 30 volts and the 54/7416 minimum output breakdown is 15 volts.

SCHEMATIC (each inverter)

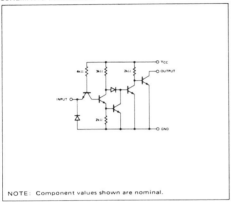

NOTE: Component values shown are nominal.

PIN CONFIGURATIONS

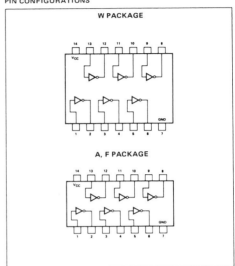

W PACKAGE

A, F PACKAGE

RECOMMENDED OPERATING CONDITIONS

	S5406, S5416			N7406, N7416			UNIT
	MIN	NOM	MAX	MIN	NOM	MAX	
Supply Voltage V_{CC}	4.5	5	5.5	4.75	5	5.25	V
Output Voltage, V_{OH}: S5406, N7406			30			30	
S5416, N7416			15			15	V
Low-level output current, I_{OL}			30			40	mA
Operating Free-air Temperature Range, T_A	−55	25	125	0	25	70	°C

ELECTRICAL CHARACTERISTICS (over recommended operating free-air temperature range unless otherwise noted)

PARAMETER		TEST CONDITIONS*	MIN	TYP**	MAX	UNIT
V_{IH}	High-level input voltage		2			V
V_{IL}	Low-level input voltage				0.8	V
I_{OH}	High-level output current	V_{CC} = MIN, V_I = 0.8V, V_{OH} = MAX			250	μA
V_{OL}	Low-level output voltage	V_{CC} = MIN, V_I = 2V, I_{OL} = MAX			0.7	V
		V_{CC} = MIN, V_I = 2V, I_{OL} = 16mA			0.4	V
I_{IH}	High-level input current (each input)	V_{CC} = MAX, V_I = 2.4V			40	μA
		V_{CC} = MAX, V_I = 5.5V			1	mA
I_{IL}	Low-level input current (each input)	V_{CC} = MAX, V_I = 0.4V			−1.6	mA
I_{CCH}	Supply current, high-level output	V_{CC} = MAX, V_I = 0		30	42	mA
I_{CCL}	Supply current, low-level output	V_{CC} = MAX, V_I = 5V		27	38	mA

Figure 3−6 Open-collector circuit bus driver. (Copyright Signetics Corp., reprinted by permission.)

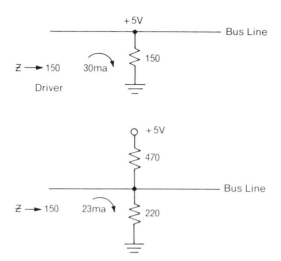

Figure 3–7   Matching bus line impedance.

SYSTEM BUSES

The *system bus* interconnects the various printed circuit (PC) boards that contain the circuits (chips) of the microprocessor family. If only a single board is required, there is no system bus problem, and many microcomputer manufacturers do supply such single-board systems. Several boards used together are usually mounted physically in a cage or crate (Figure 3-8) into which they slide or are plugged into a *motherboard*. Usually PC fingers at one edge of the board mate with connectors attached to the rear of the card cage. The wiring between these connectors, the backplane wiring, includes the system bus cables. This system normally also supplies power to the cards.

Before different cards can be interconnected in a system bus, they must meet three different standards: physical, functional, and electrical. Physically, the card terminals must mate to the cage connectors or to the motherboard. Only one edge of a card fits into the connector, and the length of this edge is the critical dimension determining the number and spacing of the connections.

It is obvious that the system bus is a parallel pathway for data bits, since it is an extension of the internal chip buses.

The function of the pins and their relative layout are very important to the performance of the bus; they may severely limit the speed and bandwidth of data transfer, for example. The number of pins can be as high as 122, but it is quite possible to have a flexible arrangement with as few as 44 pins. The important functions to provide are the address lines (usually 16), 8 pins of bidirectional data lines (to and from the ports), control and interrupt lines, and lines for power and for ground. Usually several parallel ground lines are included in a system bus.

According to a recent count,[1] 56 single-board computers and 35 different bus structures are currently being manufactured. However, only a few of these are supported by peripheral manufacturers. If you use an unsupported system bus, you may have to design and build all your own boards for such functions as floppy disk drives instead of being able to purchase them off-the-shelf. In this case you will be forced to use blank or *kluge* boards that physically match the system connectors. Thus there are advantages to using a popular or standard system bus.

The inverse of this reasoning tells why many of the detailed specifications of system buses used by large manufacturers are not publicized. The information is kept proprietary to discourage small or marginal manufacturers of plug-compatible peripheral equipment. For example, details have not been published for the IBM bus. Likewise, the Digital Equipment Corporation (DEC) Unibus is patented, and can only be used on payment of a license fee. Some other system buses that are widely used and for which information is available are the following: LSI-11; Multibus; STD bus; S-100 bus; IEEE-488; CAMAC.

Figure 3–8   Microprocessor system mounted in card cage. (Courtesy of Honeywell, Inc.)

The physical and electrical specifications of some of these systems are shown in Table 3-1. The following is a brief overview of those types, and a subsequent discussion covers the significance and impact of the differences in bus structures on the design and application of systems.

The LSI-11, for example, is a scaled-down version of the proprietary Unibus, and is limited to the LSI-11 family of microprocessors, such as the LSI-11/23. It accommodates four sizes of cards, with pin counts ranging from 36 to 144. The address and data lines are multiplexed, which releases a number of pins as spares for special uses.

The Multibus has a much wider following and has been used on more than 100 peripheral board types. It was originally designed by Intel for their 8-bit computers, but has been extended to 16-bit processors also. Since it uses a larger 12-inch board, it is more expensive to use, but the greater area also permits more freedom in the use of chips and circuitry. The major limitation of the Multibus has been its exclusive application to Intel and National Semiconductor chips. However (see next section), steps are being taken to widen its application.

The STD bus was instigated by the microprocessor manufacturer Mostek and the microcomputer firm Pro-Log to permit the use of the Z-80 and M6800 microprocessors as well as the 8080 and 8085A types. The 56-pin bus has been neatly divided into logic power, data addresses, control, and power pin groups. As indicated by Table 3-1, this system utilizes a small and inexpensive card size, so the user need only pay for immediate needs.

Unquestionably, the most popular system bus has been the S-100, the favorite of home computer hobbyists, among others. Over 400 types of boards are implemented in S-100. It was not the original intention of the originating firm, MITS, to produce a standard, but the popularity of the Altair 8800 home computer, for which it was designed, caused it to become an ad hoc standard. MITS claims no responsibility for its use by others, and specifications from many different sources have become conflicting. For example, because voltage inputs are not standard, separate board regulators may be required. Part of the popularity of the system among hobbyists results from the large number of spare lines (16), which permits the implementation of all sorts of custom designs.

STANDARDIZATION OF SYSTEM BUSES

Much confusion has been caused by the fact that none of the system buses mentioned has achieved more than de facto status as a standard, and that they have all been applied in various ways by different man-

Table 3-1   Popular Microcomputer Buses

Bus:	LSI-11	Multibus	STD Bus	S-100
Originator:	Digital Equipment Corp.	Intel	Pro-Log	MITS
Dimensions:				
Width (in.)	5.2, 10.4, 15.6	12	4.5	10.5
Height (in.)	8.4	6.75	6.5	6.5
Connector:				
Pins	72	86	56	100
Signals:				
Data	18	16	8	16
Address	18	16	16	16
Control	18	15	22	38
Interrupts	4	8	3	8
Grounds	8	8	4	2
Spares	15	7	0	16
Power	9	16	6	4
Voltages:	$\pm 5, \pm 12$	$\pm 5, \pm 12$	$\pm 5, \pm 12$	$+8, +16$

Source: Ref. 1.

ufacturers. To the user there is an obvious advantage in agreement on a single set of standards, since the user has no real assurance that two boards of the same system bus from different manufacturers will work together. Several standardizing organizations have worked toward the alleviation of this problem; the Institute of Electrical and Electronic Engineers (IEEE) has studied the S-100 to convert it to a personal computer bus standard. Incompatibility between boards built for the original 8080 and those for other microprocessors has been largely removed. Requirements of systems of increased size have also led to the provision of more adequate grounding and improved drive specifications. Data and I/0 port address lines are expanded to allow addresses up to 24 bits. Other provisions include *direct memory access* (DMA) and the definition of a *protocol* or set of rules that will arbitrate between several boards wishing to use the bus simultaneously (*bus mastership*).[2]

New standards have also been prepared for the Intel Multibus and the National Semiconductor Microbus. The Multibus has become the de facto standard for many commercial and industrial applications, just as the S-100 has appealed to personal computer designers. Changes include the expansion of the address lines to match the specifications of the 16-bit 8086 microprocessor, thus permitting both 8- and 16-bit systems to share a common bus.

PARALLEL DATA HIGHWAYS

We have only considered signal pathways that involve multiple parallel lines, one for each bit of data, and that extend for relatively short distances, at most a few feet. At this point we should consider the external pathway, the *data highway*, which is the bus that conducts information from the microcomputer central processing unit (CPU) to peripherals such as terminals, CRT displays, mass memories, or control devices and sensors. These may be a few tens or hundreds of feet distant, or even thousands of feet, as in the case of industrial control or data acquisition systems. It is even possible for microcomputers to communicate over thousands of miles, sometimes via space satellites.

There are two basic types of signal transmission: parallel, as defined above, and serial. In the latter only one signal line is needed, and the bits in a word are sent sequentially, one at a time. Parallel systems are faster for obvious reasons. In the number of clock periods required for a serial system to transmit a single bit of information, an 8-line parallel system can send an entire symbol, word, or byte. [The unit of speed of information transfer in terms of symbols per second is called the *baud*, named after J. Baudot, an early French telegraphic scientist. The American Standard Code for Information Exchange (ASCII, see Table 3-2) represents alphanumeric and special characters by the use of 7 bits, hence the bit rate for ASCII code without redundancy is 7 times the symbol or baud rate. For binary symbols the baud and bit rates are equal.]

The speed advantage of parallel transmission clearly carries with it the penalty of greater cost, since one channel is required for each parallel bit. In terms of wire and connector pins (or of bandwidth in coaxial and radio media) it is easy to account for this cost. A more subtle penalty also exists, however, because of the finite and variable speed of bits in each channel. Like the effect of capacitance discussed earlier in this chapter, slight differences in signal path or media unsynchronize the bits making up the symbol so that they do not all arrive at their destination at identical times. At high transmission rates, on the order of a megabit/second or more, this effect becomes important in cables a few tens or hundreds of feet in length. The design of signal control apparatus and the signals themselves to minimize this distortion is a sophisticated art. Nevertheless, parallel highways are very useful and widely used for interconnecting instruments in the same room and for other short-distance applications.

The first standard parallel bus system, now called IEEE-488 instrument bus, was developed by Hewlett-Packard to interconnect its minicomputers with electronic bench test instrumentation. The IEEE

				high b_7	0	0	0	0	1	1	1	1
				bits b_6	0	0	1	1	0	0	1	1
low bits				b_5	0	1	0	1	0	1	0	1
b_4	b_3	b_2	b_1	HEX	0	1	2	3	4	5	6	7
0	0	0	0	0	NUL	DLE	SP	0	@	P		p
0	0	0	1	1	SOH	DC1	!	1	A	Q	a	q
0	0	1	0	2	STX	DC2	"	2	B	R	b	r
0	0	1	1	3	ETX	DC3	#	3	C	S	c	s
0	1	0	0	4	EOT	DC4	$	4	D	T	d	t
0	1	0	1	5	ENQ	NAK	%	5	E	U	e	u
0	1	1	0	6	ACK	SYN	&	6	F	V	f	v
0	1	1	1	7	BEL	ETB	'	7	G	W	g	w
1	0	0	0	8	BS	CAN	(	8	H	X	h	x
1	0	0	1	9	HT	EM	)	9	I	Y	i	y
1	0	1	0	A	LF	SUB	*	:	J	Z	j	z
1	0	1	1	B	VT	ESC	+	;	K	[	k	{
1	1	0	0	C	FF	FS	,	<	L	\	l	|
1	1	0	1	D	CR	GS	-	=	M	]	m	}
1	1	1	0	E	SO	RS	.	>	N	^	n	~
1	1	1	1	F	SI	US	/	?	O	——	o	DEL

Table 3–2   American Standard Code for Information Exchange (ASCII).

and the American National Standards Institute (ANSI) adopted the system as a standard in 1977. Subsequently, it was recognized in substantially the same form by the International Electrotechnical Commission (IEC). The IEEE-488 (see Table 3-3) is designed for interconnection within the relatively small area of the laboratory, and is consequently limited to 20 meters. A more typical distance is 5 meters. Baud rates in noisefree environments can range from 100K bytes/second to as high as 2 megabytes/second, with longer lines permitted at the lower baud rates.

The 24-conductor cable consists of a data bus of eight lines, three lines for control of data byte transfer, and five for general control of the interface between the processors and instruments. A 24-pin plug is specified in the IEEE standard; this plug has special male-female mating provisions that allow up to 15 devices to be arranged in a ring or loop. The connectors in the American and European versions differ in this regard.

Although any 8-bit data can be transferred over this bus, there is no assurance that the byte will be meaningful to the recipient. This problem introduces a whole new set of difficulties in communication standardization known as *protocol*. Protocol is a set of rules that specifies such things as the designation of talkers and listeners, who can use the line (the bus master), what constitutes the beginning and end of the message, how to detect errors and what to do to recover from them, and at the highest level, the application software or meaning of the data. Protocol is even more important in the case of serial transmission and in cases involving more than two stations; however, we defer these complexities to a subsequent discussion.

The only other parallel bus standard of general significance at this writing is the CAMAC (computer automated measurement and control). The CAMAC uses a cable of 86 conductors, compared to the 24 of the IEEE-488, but has the advantage of a much higher transmission speed (5 megabytes/second maximum). Typically, a CAMAC bus can extend about 1,000 feet, but with the baud rate limited to around 500K this can be extended to nearly a mile. Details can be found in IEEE Standards 583, 595, and 596 (see also Table 3-3).

Because of the large cable, CAMAC is a very expensive way of doing things. It has been said to be overspecified,[1] in part because of the complex crate with room for 25 modules. Its primary use is in the nuclear power industry.

SERIAL DATA TRANSMISSION

When digital data are bit serial, transmitted one bit at a time (as distinguished from the byte-serial, bit-parallel systems just discussed), multiple-channel media and multiple-conductor cables are not needed, and elaborate and expensive connectors are simplified. The bits can be sent over any electrical path such as a pair of wires, a coaxial cable, or telephone lines, or with proper interface the media may be radio and microwave, light (as in fiber optics cables), infrared, or sound. The telephone dial network is a well-known example of a serial communication channel. Transmission speeds in the broad-band media such as microwave and fiber optics may be hundreds of megacycles, while several megacycles or megabits is common in coaxial cable (e.g., cable TV). Thus the apparent speed advantage of parallel bus highways tends to disappear in practice, particularly if long paths are required.

The bit-at-a-time nature of serial transmission also alleviates the synchronization problem and allows the use of longer paths. Even with propagation delays of many tens of microseconds, as with coaxial cable, or the milliseconds experienced with satellite communication, separate bits can be recognized because each is delayed by the same amount. However, a somewhat different problem arises, since a binary signal, nominally a square wave, contains a broad band of frequencies (theoretically infinite). In any real transmission medium of limited bandwidth, such as coaxial cable, each of these frequencies is transmitted at different speeds, with the result that with increasing distance the signal becomes distorted, usually rounded and flattened or spread out in the time dimension.[3] Thus it becomes difficult to detect the beginning and end of a bit or which bit is a *mark* (ONE) or *space* (ZERO). This problem is called *intersymbol interference* (Figure 3-9), and is alleviated by careful design of the transmission line and drivers and by specially shaping the signal itself.[4] Intersymbol interference exists even in the absence of noise, since it is a consequence of the limitation in band-

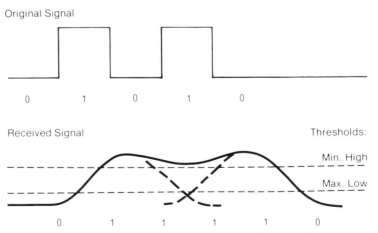

Figure 3–9   Intersymbol interference (waveform distortion) resulting from bandwidth limitation of transmission medium.

width. Consequently, it is most noticeable in twisted pairs and increasingly less so in coaxial cable, microwave, or optical media.

Table 3-4 exhibits the characteristics of several serial standards and media commonly used with microprocessor systems. Of these the most elementary and earliest is the TTY or *current loop*. TTY is derived from its original application to teletypewriters. "Current loop" describes the form of signal that is the presence (ONE) or absence (ZERO) of a 20-milliampere current flow in a signal-ground pair of wires. Since in any electrical circuit the time for current buildup to a fixed point, such as 20 milliamperes, is a function of line inductance, capacitance and resistance (time constant), and the driving voltage, TTY is inherently limited in line length (affecting time constant) and rate of transmission, or both. Recommended limits are 4800 bits/second (baud) and 2000 feet, with 100 bits/second and 1000 feet being perhaps more typical. A specific industrial system, for example, is 5000 feet long and allows a 20-microsecond rise time for the current pulse.

Usually TTY transmission lines are balanced (nongrounded) twisted wire pairs. In addition, the elementary TTY waveform is *baseband*, meaning that it is basically a dc signal. The alternative is a modulated signal, in which the baseband symbol modulates some characteristic of an oscillating wave, for example, its frequency (fm), amplitude (am), or phase (pm). At a later point we consider such modulated systems, called *carriers*. At this point we note that such a modulation-demodulation (*modem*) technique is required if TTY is to be extended for more than a mile at rates of over a few hundred baud. The basic idea of the modem is to modulate an audio frequency waveform with the baseband signal, either in amplitude, frequency, or phase. Two of the most popular

Table 3-3   External Data Buses—Parallel

	IEEE-488	CAMAC
Format	Parallel	Parallel
Conductors	24	86
Typical data rate	100K bytes/s	1M bytes/s
Maximum data rate	2M bytes/s	5M bytes/s
Typical cable length	5 in	1,000 ft[a]
Maximum cable length	20 in	5,500 ft[a]
		@ 500K baud
Typical signaling	TTL	Biphase NRZ

Source: Ref. 1.
[a]Using CAMAC serial dataway.

modem techniques are shift between two frequencies, representing mark and space, called *frequency shift keying* (FSK), and a similar shift between two opposite phases, *phase shift keying* (PSK). The modulated waveform can be electrically or acoustically coupled to the common-carrier telephone lines. The ubiquitous telephone handset couplers that accompany many computer terminals, teletypewriters, and CRT stations are examples of this usage. In addition, there are modem chips that are compatible with microprocessors, such as the Motorola MC6860, a 600-bit-per-second FSK circuit.

RS-232   INTERFACE

The RS-232 interface is a standard parallel-to-serial interface most commonly supplied with single-board microcomputers and low-speed peripherals of all types. It was initially developed by the Electronic Industries Association (EIA) (RS-232C) to standardize the connection of computers with telephone line modems, and has been adopted for this purpose by the Bell Telephone Company. In fact, this standard has become so identified with Bell modems that the Cinch DB-25 connector used by Bell, though not an official part of the EIA standard, has become universally associated with the RS-232 (Figure 3-10).

The standard allows as many as 20 signals to be defined, but gives complete freedom to the user. In practice three wires are sufficient: send

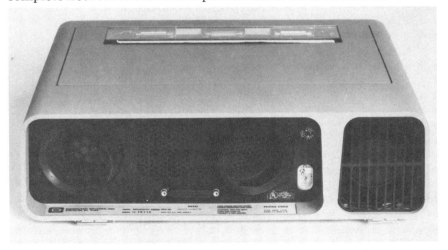

Figure 3–10   Acoustic modem and RS-232 interface. (Copyright Computer Devices, Inc., reprinted by permission.)

data, receive data, and signal ground. The remaining lines can be hard-wired on or off permanently. The signal transmission is bipolar, requiring two voltages, from 5 to 25 volts, of opposite polarity. This requirement is an obsolete hangover from electron tube days and is not compatible with the needs of TTL logic levels. Hence there have been some attempts to update this specification electrically (EIA RS-422 for balanced lines and RS-433 for unbalanced), but the popularity of the older standard has resulted in resistance to the change—only a few terminals actually use them.

UART

The actual conversion of parallel-to-serial data is accomplished by the universal asynchronous receiver transmitter (UART). This simple means of converting between 8-bit computer format and serial TTY can be constructed from a few logic chips. However, there is no need to do this, since the UART TTY interface, which also includes timing control circuitry, was one of the first to be placed on a single integrated chip.[5] It has even been included in some of the new single-chip microprocessors as an integrated function.

Figure 3-11 shows a typical UART functional block diagram. Separate transmit and receive paths to the serial bus are provided. The

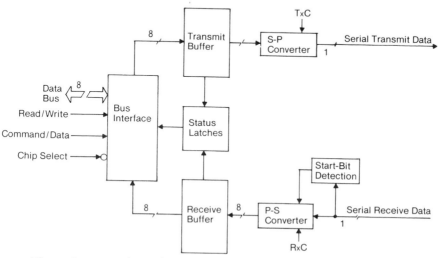

Figure 3–11   Universal synchronous receiver-transmitter (UART).

computer 8-bit bus and control lines are connected to the UART computer bus interface section. If the computer wishes to transmit, it places an 8-bit byte on its data bus lines and sends a WRITE command to the UART via the control lines. This action causes the byte to be transferred to the transmit buffer section, where it is held until the serial line is free and then shifted to the parallel-serial converter. This device first adds start and stop bits to either end of the byte (part of the TTY protocol) and then, under control of the transmit clock (TC), sends the bits out one at a time on the serial transmit bus (transmit data).

To receive, the procedure is reversed. A start bit is detected on the receive data serial line, stimulating the UART to assemble a byte of data in the 8-bit receive buffer, having first undergone a serial-parallel conversion. It is held there until a READ command is sent by the computer, at which time it is shifted out to the computer data bus through the UART bus interface.

The UART can accept another byte of data from the CPU while it is still transmitting the first byte. The status latch associated with the transmit buffer is set as soon as the byte is transferred to the converter, and this action can be interpreted by the computer as an invitation to send the next byte. Similarly, there is a receive latch whose set status signifies that a character has been received, and can signal the computer to accept it. Since transmission and reception can be accomplished at

Table 3-4   External Data Buses—Serial

	RS-232	RS-449	TTY	Twisted-Pair Twin Axial	Coax
Format	Serial	Serial	Serial	Serial	Serial
Conductors	25	37	6	2	2
Typical data rate	9600 baud	100K baud	110 baud	9600 baud	1.5M baud
Maximum data rate	20K baud	2M baud	4800 baud	500K baud	5M baud
Typical cable length	10 ft	10 ft	1000 ft	1 mi	1 mi
Maximum cable length	50 ft	50 ft	10,000 ft @ 400 baud	6 mi	2 mi
Typical signaling	Bipolar	Bipolar	Current	Baseband FSK	FSK PSK biphase

Source: Ref. 1.

any time, the line is not in use through the agency of these status latches, and synchronism between transmitter and receiver is unnecessary. Hence the UART is *asynchronous*. These status signals further adapt very conveniently to an interrupt mode of processor operation.

The three signals used by the CPU to control the UART are commonly contained in the two address bytes and are decoded by the UART interface from the CPU address bus. The *chip select* address is used to enable the UART to receive computer data, as well as identify it if there are more than one. It appears on the higher order address byte. A bit in the lower address byte identifies command or status information if it is a ONE or data if it is ZERO. The read/write line responds to an input or output instruction from the CPU: ONE for input and ZERO for output.

Since the RS-232 voltage levels are not consistent with microprocessor logic, external hardware is needed to convert between them. This has caused the development of special UART IC chips by microprocessor manufacturers that render this conversion unnecessary. One such chip is the Motorola 6851 asynchronous communications interface adapter (ACIA), which is a conventional UART compatible with the Motorola M6800 microprocessor family. Another is the Intel 8251 USART, which combines both asynchronous and synchronous communication capability. These chips can be used freely to interconnect their microprocessors with outside terminals and peripherals accepting TTY format.

RS-449 EXTERNAL BUS

The slow speed of the RS-232 makes it inapplicable to peripherals operating at more than 10 or 20 thousand bits per second, generally considered low-speed data transfer devices. Thus TTY is adequate for many keyboards, terminals, and printers, but for loading programs into memory and for data interchange between computers, higher speeds are required. The major advantage of the RS-449 is that it allows serial transmission of up to 2 megabits/second, 100 times the RS-232 limit. This standard requires a 37-pin connector for a single channel and a supplementary 9-pin connector for two. The additional expense and complexity have inhibited acceptance of this standard on the same level as the RS-232. The result is that most high-speed data transfer systems are designs unique to a single manufacturer. However, there is currently much activity to develop such standards in both American and European organizations, largely as a result of the increased use of data highways in industry and the rising tide of digital communication on common carriers.

TWO-WIRE VERSUS COAXIAL CABLE

For local transmission (neglecting the telephone system, which is a special situation) the practical choice is between twisted pairs and coaxial cable for serial communication. Optical fibers promise very high performance, but are much more difficult to splice and interconnect than copper wires. For the present we are mostly concerned with the trade-off between two-wire cables (twisted pair or twin-axial) and coaxial cable.

Twisted pairs serve adequately for TTY communication lines, and have been used at speeds approaching 0.5 megabits per second and for distances of several miles, at slower rates. Baseband (DC) signaling is adequate for the shorter distance, and FSK modems extend the range for more demanding applications.

At speeds permitted by the RS-449, coaxial cable or similar broadband media are required. Coaxial cable also gives inherently better shielding against the electrical noise characteristic of industrial environments. Typically, a 1-megabit-per-second baseband signal can be transmitted over 5000 feet of coaxial cable, assuming that it is properly terminated with its characteristic impedance (usually a 70-ohm resistor). Noise pickup under these conditions is negligible. With repeaters this distance can be extended several times, or modems can be used to increase the speed to as much as 5 megabits per second and the line length to 10,000 feet.

REFERENCES

1   McGowan, M. J., *Control Engineering*, 31–34 (April 1977).
2   Allison, A., *Mini-Micro Systems*, **12**, 66–69 (October 1979).
3   Bennet, W. R., and Davey, J. R., *Data Transmission*, New York: McGraw-Hill (1965).
4   Reference 3, pp. 96–98.
5   Ogdin, C. A., *Mini-Micro Systems*, **11**, 95–104 (November 1978).

4

High Level Programming with Microcomputers—BASIC

REASONS FOR HIGH LEVEL PROGRAMMING

If we want a microprocessor to perform some function that is useful to us, whether it is to play tic-tac-toe or to control a process or a household task, it must first be programmed. The general idea of computer programs and the steps used to generate them are shown in Chapter 2, which also introduces the concepts of assembly and higher level languages as well as some of the reasons for choosing each. In this chapter we show some of the actual steps used to develop programs in a high level language, BASIC. Because microprocessors are becoming more powerful and memory is decreasing in cost, higher level languages are becoming more practical and their use will accelerate in the future.

Furthermore, software development costs, an essential part of microprocessor applications, are becoming extremely high,[3] about $20 per line, independent of the programming language. Since high level languages are more "natural," they are easier to use than are assembly level languages, and it is also easier to create, correct, and modify programs. Since a line of high level language is the equivalent of several lines of assembly language, program development costs are substantially lower.

One objection to using high level languages is the cost of memory. A user who wishes to develop programs, that is, who uses a microprocessor as a computer, with appropriate input and output (keyboard and CRT or printer, as in a home computer), must allocate RAM or ROM memory space for a program to convert the high level language, whatever it may be, to binary form so that it can be used by the CPU. This space is typically 3 to 8K or even more for a *compiler* or *interpreter* used with microprocessors (see *Programming in BASIC*, page 89, for a discussion of these two methods). For the home user these objections are overcome by the enormous convenience of being able to converse more naturally with the machine. The availability of increased memory space and the plummeting cost of MSI/LSI memory support this conclusion. The professional microprocessor device developer may not need a resident interpreter, since his programs are written in ROM and are not altered by the user. ROM programs (firmware) are created using development systems, as shown in Chapter 2; these systems are off-line and may even be large computers. The end product of the process is binary ROM, which is directly intelligible to the computer. Nevertheless, there is an objection by some that ROM developed from high level languages is less efficient; that is, it uses more machine level statements for a given function than "hand-coded" assembly programming. In large-scale production of microprocessor-based devices where memory is still a substantial cost (perhaps $40 to $80 per 16K of RAM) and may become a major factor in total production costs, this is a serious problem. But even in these cases the ease of coding and debugging and the superior ability to upgrade devices by reprogramming (using replaceable ROM or PROM) usually outweigh the added memory cost. Again, the lowering of memory cost plus the development of more efficient compilers and languages favor the choice of high level programming.

In this chapter we describe the use of BASIC, the original and commonest language for small computers. It also serves as a model for other languages available to microprocessor users, and some of these are discussed further on.

PROGRAMMING IN GENERAL

Computer programming is a constructive mental process, somewhat like solving crossword puzzles or cryptograms. As such, it is an individualistic process. If two skilled programmers are given a complex task, they will seldom arrive at identical programs, although both will be "correct." Because the computer is such a complex device and has so many states, there are many paths that lead to the same conclusion.

Therefore the temptation for new programmers is to be ingenious, subtle, and individualistic, and to continually reinvent rounder and rounder wheels. Experience teaches us, however, that programming is a time-consuming and expensive process. Almost all programs have logical errors to begin with, and must be debugged or updated, not always by the originator. Furthermore, programs must be understood by others if they are to be properly applied. Therefore it pays to be simple, straightforward, orderly, and to use proven, standard methods and procedures as much as possible. "Structured" programming, starting with the larger-scale objectives and working down to the details, is much to be desired. Where teams of programmers work together in a common project, structured and "egoless" programming is a necessity. Even the individual worker at home or in the laboratory will profit by an orderly, structured approach to program generation and future maintenance or modification.

The steps that facilitate an orderly approach to programming are

Top-down structuring.
Flowcharting.
Algorithm development.
Higher order languages.

For reasons of efficiency in use of memory and product cost minimization, the use of assembly language programming may be necessary instead. This decision must be a trade-off between the cost of programming in terms of economics or effort versus the cost of saved memory.

FLOWCHARTS AND ALGORITHMS

A flowchart is a graphical portrait of a procedure for accomplishing a task in some detail. In top-down programming there may be several successive steps in flowcharting, starting with a very broad view of the task and working down into finer detail. At the lowest level coding takes over, and for higher level languages it may not be necessary to flowchart past a rather broad view of the task. The purpose of flowcharting is to describe the details of the task accurately enough so that they can be converted to computer instructions, and to be certain that they are completely logical and self-consistent, taking into account the full range of conditions being considered. For example, if one step in a computing procedure involves finding a square root and the input may become negative during the program, it must be decided what should be done in that case or how to interpret a negative square root.

An algorithm is a precise and detailed procedure for accomplishing a task, a set of rigorous rules in a well-defined language which are simple enough to be accomplished by a machine. A computer program is an algorithm, therefore, but the word refers to the mental construct or concept, not to the particular language in which it is implemented. The words "method," "procedure," and "recipe" are almost synonymous. Therefore an algorithm can implement the task of a flowchart and precede (or be synonymous with) a program. Before choosing a language in which to code your program, you can make up your own "plain language" statements, so long as you define each term exactly. This procedure is dignified by the term *pseudocode*, and is used by professionals to represent, let us say, a statement in a new language that has not yet been developed or machine code in a computer that has not yet been built.

As a concrete example let us take a part of the benchmark task used in Chapter 2 for comparing the effectiveness of several microprocessors, the table lookup. Let us assume that we have in memory a table of N numbers placed in sequential locations, and that we wish to search this table to find the location j of a specific input number X. The top level or overview of this operation can be flowcharted as in Figure 4-1. This describes in general what we want to accomplish in a standard symbology. The diamond, for example, indicates a decision, question, or comparison that can be answered as "yes" or "no." In programming parlance this is called a *branch*, since the subsequent action of the algorithm "branches" or depends on the outcome. This level of flowcharting is informative, but is not suitable for algorithm development or coding

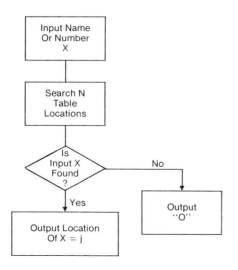

Figure 4–1   Table search overview flowchart.

because it lacks sufficient detail and the operations are not rigorously defined. For example, how do we actually search the table? There are many ways of doing this; each results in a different algorithm, and some algorithms are perhaps more suitable than others for a given task (e.g., they may differ in execution speed).

The search task described need not be trivial or restricted to numbers. The numbers in the table may represent parts in a stock list or even names of people or objects in some alphabetical code such as ASCII. In this code each symbol is represented by a 7-bit binary code (see Table 3-2); for example, the uppercase letters A, B, . . . , Z are (translated to octal) 101, 102, . . . , 132. Thus the name "BROWN" can be translated as 102, 122, 117, 127, 116 (octal) and stored in 15 sequential bytes of storage. Our task, then, can represent an elementary information retrieval system.

In this program we are not concerned with how the items were input to storage in the first place. In this first case the order in which they appear is also unimportant. (However, it is ultimately necessary for the machine to know how many bytes of storage are used to represent a name or *key*, the item to be searched in the table.)

For the first stage let us assume that we will attempt a "brute force" or sequential search of the table. That is, store one key record in each of the locations 1 to N. We compare each key with the input X (where X = "BROWN," for example) until we find a match, then output the address j of the location where X was found. If X is not found after searching all N locations, the address "0" is to be output, representing failure of the search.

An algorithm by definition must be precise and also take into account all important contingencies. It cannot be assumed that the machine has any "intelligence" except what we put into it in the form of the algorithm. In this task we want to be able to search a list of any length (up to some maximum set by our problem and the available hardware); in other words N is an input variable; N may also be zero. For the moment we are not concerned about the actual method of comparing X with the KEY (j), the value of the key word stored at address j, since this depends on the hardware or the available instruction set. However, it is easy to see that if X and KEY (j) were both 1 byte, they could be compared by subtracting one from the other and seeing if the result was zero.

Donald E. Knuth, a professor at Stanford University and one of the leading practitioners of the art of algorithm design, has offered the following as a solution to this search problem:[1]

1   (Initialize.) Set j ← N. [*Remarks:* N is the number of words in the
    sequential table. We assume that it is also the address of the last
    word in the table, though, of course, there could be an offset A in the
    address. The algorithm searches each address from N to 0 and
    outputs 0 unless it finds the input word X first, in which case it
    outputs the address j where X was found. *Note:* The backward arrow
    means "set (j) equal to (N)." This symbol avoids confusion with the
    equal sign, which tests for equality.]
2   Unsuccessful? If j = 0, output j and terminate the algorithm.
    (Otherwise continue to the next step.)
3   Successful? If X = KEY (j), output j and terminate the algorithm.
    (Otherwise continue to the next step.)
4   Repeat. Set j ← j − 1 (i.e., decrease the current value of j by 1) and go
    back to Step 2.

   This algorithm is flowcharted in Figure 4-2, and the logic is laid out
very clearly in this graph. It can be seen by following through the
sequence indicated by arrows that all the requirements are met. The
algorithm steps down each address searching for X in KEY (j) and, when
it is found, outputs j and stops. Whenever the end of the table is reached
without finding X, the value j = 0 is output.

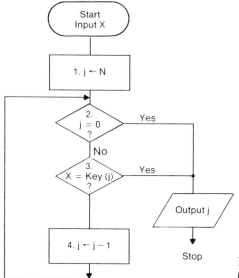

Figure 4–2   Table search algorithm.
(After D. Knuth, Ref. 1.)

It is true that this is a very simple and naive way to search a table. If there are 10,000 entries, 10,000 iterations of Steps 3 and 4 are required in the worst case (where X is not in the table). On the average it requires 5000 iterations. A much better way of doing this job is *binary search*. In this method all the keys are stored in order of their size; that is, KEY (j) is a smaller number than KEY (j + 1).

Dividing the list in two, we can determine (by comparing X with the boundaries) which half contains X. Knuth has shown that the number of comparisons required is only k, the smallest integer such that 2^k is greater than N; thus k = 14 for N = 10,000, a tremendous saving. The algorithm for binary search is somewhat more complex than the brute force method and conceptually more difficult. (The reader is urged to try to construct this algorithm. The answer can be found in Knuth's article.[1])

PROGRAMMING IN BASIC

The development of a successful algorithm is a necessary but not sufficient step toward the goal of instructing the computer to perform the job. The next task is to convert the algorithm to a program that can eventually be stored in program memory. In this chapter we concentrate on higher level languages that are more suited to the problem and fit more easily into human thought patterns than machine language or even the mnemonics of assembly languages. The best known of these is BASIC, an abbreviation for *B*eginner's *A*ll-purpose *S*ymbolic *I*nstruction *C*ode, a language developed at Dartmouth College in 1965 and now used almost universally on both large and small computers. There is no one BASIC language, but something like 90 different versions or dialects;[2] however, all have certain common features that make it easy to use any version once the fundamentals are mastered. Since BASIC is job and human oriented, it cannot be understood by the computer as written, but must go through the intermediate step of a compiler or interpreter, as explained in Chapter 2. As far as the programmer is concerned, it makes very little difference whether a compiler or interpreter is used. A compiler, generally used in a large computer, converts the source program written in BASIC to an object program or file in machine language which is then stored in memory. This is usually done in one pass, hence the name *one-pass compiler*, which is often used. (Some more sophisticated languages use a more complicated procedure.) In the compiler each BASIC phrase or statement is converted to one or more machine instructions. An interpreter is similar in result, but the conversion is usually done while the program is running, one statement at a time. The difference between the two, which is important to the microprocessor user, is that the interpreter must be present in memory while the program is being run, while the compiler can be removed once it has done its job. Thus there is a memory penalty to using an interpreter, usually a minimum of 4 or 8K for the more sophisticated versions. One would think then that a microcomputer would most often use a compiler, but this is not the case. Since interpreter programs can be run line-by-line, they can be debugged simply rather than being recompiled for each correction, and they are more popular in small computers. In certain versions, such as the Synertek BAS-1, the interpreter is stored in ROM, which is less expensive than RAM, and does not need to be loaded from some external source such as a cassette.

We have stated that BASIC is well matched to human thinking, and we can further characterize it as having an Englishlike structure that is *almost* immediately comprehensible to anyone familiar with high school algebra.

Perhaps the best way to demonstrate this is to go through an actual case and point out the features as they occur. As an example we continue with the searching algorithm developed in Figure 4-2. This is correct and proper, since flowcharting should precede programming or coding in a job of any complexity. In fact, BASIC is so easy to learn that the flowchart can be coded almost directly.

Let us assume, as a concrete example, that we have 10 names in a list. Associated with each name is a number; for simplicity we use the decimal number that is the ASCII code for the first initial. (Of course, we could convert the entire name to ASCII code at the cost of 1 byte per letter or, as explained subsequently, use the names directly, but to keep things simple we use only one two-digit number per name.) The list looks like the following:

Address	Name	ASCII (Decimal Code)
1	JONES	74
2	SMITH	83
3	BROWN	66
4	CLARK	67
5	WILLIAMS	87
6	ABLES	65
7	THOMAS	84
8	PERKINS	80
9	LALLY	76
10	FRIEND	70

In BASIC the algorithm of Figure 4-2 can be written as follows:

```
  1 REM THIS PROGRAM SEARCHES A LIST AND PRINTS THE
    ADDRESS
 10 DATA 74, 83, 66, 67, 87, 65, 84, 80, 76, 70
 20 LET N = 10
 30 LET X = 65
 40 LET J = N
 50 IF J = 0 GO TO 100
 60 READ K
 70 IF K = X GO TO 100
 80 LET J = J − 1
 90 GO TO 50
100 PRINT J
110 END
```

Already this program makes a certain amount of sense to the reader. After a line explaining what the program is to do (line 1), we start (line 10) with a list that is obviously the name codes we are about to search. Appropriately this is called *DATA*. Then (line 20) we set forth the value of N, the number of items in the list. In line 30, X is the item (code) we are searching for, decimal 65 or the letter "A."

In line 40 we begin the algorithm of Figure 4-2 by letting J = N, or 10. If (line 50) J = 0, we GO TO or jump to 100. Looking ahead, we see that line 100 says PRINT J. This is in accordance with the algorithm's Step 2. Since J does not equal 0, it seems natural to read the next line (60), which commands the computer to READ K, where K stands for KEY (j) of Step 3, Figure 4-2. In BASIC, READ means to read sequentially, one at a time, the items in the DATA list (the items are separated by commas), so that the machine will READ 74. (The next time that we run across this READ statement it will be 83 that is read, since we have "used" 74.)

Line 70 states that we should GO TO 100 if K = X. (K and X are simple variable numbers here, but they could be more complex expressions.) Since we have READ K as 74 and originally set X = 65, the statement K = X is not true. Following our implied rule, we do *not* jump to 100, but read the next line. Line 80 is the same as Step 4 of the algorithm; that is, we assign to the value J the number that is one less than its current value, which in this case is 10. So now J = 10 − 1, or 9.

The astute reader will note that we have used the "=" sign in two different ways. In this line (and in lines 20 to 40), the = following LET means "assign" the value of *expression* on the right to the *variable* on the left. That is, the arithmetic expression N − 1 (where N is equal to 10) is evaluated, giving 9, and the variable N is now assigned this new value. In lines 20 to 40, the "expression" is merely a constant, 10 or 65 in this case. (In most versions of BASIC, the LET is optional; that is, line 80 could have been written

$$J = J - 1$$

In this case, the LET is often reserved as a means of "flagging" new variables entering the program.)

The second mode of the = sign follows the IF statement. This is used more like the conventional = of algebra, but in the IF statement we are interested in whether the *relation* between the two expressions following the IF is TRUE or FALSE. In other words, we are interested in the Boolean value of the expression following IF. In the statement "K = X" K and X can be any expressions, and the relational operator is "=." If K does indeed equal X, the Boolean value of the statement "K = X" is TRUE; otherwise it is FALSE. In the IF THEN statement, lines 50 and 70, for example, the command following THEN is obeyed only if the Boolean value is TRUE. If not, the command is ignored and the next line is read.

Continuing with the program, after decrementing J in line 80, we arrive at line 90, which is an *unconditional branch*, GO TO (line) 50. This follows the algorithm (Figure 4-2), where the address (J) decrement is followed by retesting to see whether we have reached the end of the list (J = 0) without a "hit," that is, finding a location that contains the key 65 for which we are searching. The algorithm as well as the program (lines 50 and 100) tell us to symbolize this event by printing or outputting the number "0."

In our example we continue to recycle from lines 50 to 90, reducing the address J by one each time and testing to see if K, the next data item, is 65, each time, until we reach a hit at the value J = 5. Since the relational statement of line 70 then becomes true, we GO TO 100 and print the current value of J. Thus the result of the program is simply the printout

5

meaning that our key word was found and that it was in address 5.

The above explanation treated BASIC in a somewhat wordy and intuitive manner; actually, the rules for this or any programming language must be very precise and can be stated succinctly. Unfortunately, the compact definitions are more difficult to learn than the language itself for the reader untrained in logic or symbolic algebra. We do not go into this representation but, to recapitulate, we will state the BASIC rules applying to this program with somewhat more rigor.

LINE NUMBERS

Every line of BASIC is a statement and every statement must be preceded by a line number followed by a space. Only integers are permitted. 0 is not a valid line number, but leading zeros (e.g., 007) are usually permitted. There is some upper limit on numbers; for example, 1 to 9999 are valid in Honeywell 700 BASIC.

Line numbers need not be consecutive, but statements must be numbered in ascending order and must be unique. However, lines may be entered in any order and the interpreter will automatically order the file in correct sequence. It is good programming practice to number lines in multiples of 10; then if one must later insert a line between, say, lines 40 and 50, there are nine numbers available (41 through 49) for new lines. If a line number is duplicated, BASIC substitutes the last statement for the earlier one, so this feature may be used for editing and correcting statement or typing errors.

Line numbers (ln hereafter) are also used as statement markers. In our example program GO TO 100 uses the ln as a guidepost to transfer control to statement 100.

SPACE

Following ln there must be (in many BASICs) one blank character (space). The remainder of the statement line may contain spaces or not as desired, since they are ignored by the interpreter. Thus the programmer may use spaces to make the program easier to read and more orderly or structured.

For example, the statement GO TO ln may also be written GOTO ln. Or a group of common statements may be indented to indicate their unity; for example,

```
10   Y = 10
20   FOR X = 1 TO 3
30      PRINT X
40      PRINT Y
50      Y = Y + 2
60   NEXT X
80   END
```

(The meaning of the FOR-TO statement is explained later.)

REMARKS

Any statement on a line beginning with REM is ignored by the interpreter or compiler. However, these *remarks* may be extremely valuable in explaining the purpose and method of the program in notebook fashion. Either another user or the original programmer may need a reminder of the program's salient features. Some BASIC variations use the apostrophe (') as an abbreviation for REM. It may also be used to enclose a remark in single quotes on a line that contains an active statement; for example,

100 END 'THIS IS END OF PROGRAM'

The asterisk (*) has also been used to signify a remark, but only if it appears as the first nonblank character in the statement, as:

10 *THIS IS ANOTHER REMARK

In any other position, the * is used as the multiplication operator, instead of arithmetic's "×" for "times."

DATA

We have already discussed the DATA statement. Data lines can be put anywhere in a program, and form a *pool* of data that can be READ and reused. Some BASICs allow *strings* or alphabetical data (see the section on input/output) to be put in the DATA pool

CONSTANTS

A constant is a signed number. Small microprocessor BASICs are limited to integers. If there is no sign, the constant is assumed to be positive. A floating point number, if allowable, is distinguished by a decimal point; for example,

$$-30.0 \text{ means } -.03 \times 10^2$$
$$0.24 \text{ means } 0.24 \times 10^0$$
$$.003 \text{ means } 0.3 \times 10^{-2}$$

Some BASIC compilers also permit exponential numbers, using E as a symbol for "exponent of 10." Thus

$$5.65E12 \quad \text{means } 5.65 \times 10^{12}$$
$$0.3E\text{-}2 \quad \text{means } 0.3 \times 10^{-2} \text{ or } .003$$

Constants retain their value throughout a program.

VARIABLES

Variables are those quantities that may change value during the program, such as J and K in our search example. BASIC allows any letter to be used as a variable name, or a letter followed by a single digit, 0 to 9, for a total of 260 possible names. Thus A, X, and N are legal variable names, as are A1, A2, or X9, but C3PO (too long)[a] and 3J (starts with a number instead of a letter) are not. For most programs 260 variable names are more than enough. A variable may take on any value that is permitted a constant. A variable does not need to change its value during the program; for example, N remains constant at 10 in our example. But it is convenient to use the variable construct, both for mnemonic reasons and to allow us to change the program easily if the data are changed. For example, if we want to add two data items, we merely substitute 12 for 10 in line 20 and the program will run as before.

EXPRESSIONS

Variables and constants can be combined with arithmetic symbols to

[a] Legal in some BASICs where any character after the second one is ignored.

form algebralike formulas that are called BASIC *expressions*. An example is J-1 in line 80. Another is

$$X \uparrow 2 + 3*A - 1.6$$

where $\uparrow$ represents exponentiation (i.e., X^2), * is the multiplication operator, and + and −, have their usual arithmetic meanings. The upward arrow symbol $\uparrow$ may be replaced by ** or $\wedge$ in some BASIC versions. Parentheses may be used, as in $2*(3 + X)$.

The symbols used with expressions are, in order of their priority (see below),

Operator	Meaning
$\uparrow$,$\wedge$, or **	Exponentiation
*	Multiplication or
/	Division
+	Addition and
−	Subtraction

The rules of expression formation are as follows:

1   Operators may not be adjacent; that is, $X*+2$ is illegal, but $X*(+2)$ is all right (the parenthesis is used to separate the operators).
2   Variables and constants may not be adjacent. Twice X cannot be written 2X, but $2*X$ is legal.
3   Parentheses must enclose a legal expression. Parentheses may be "nested," as in many algebraic calculations; for example,

$$A*(B+C*(D-F))$$

Note that for every opening parenthesis there must be a corresponding closing one. In complex expressions it is advisable to count them to see if they are all paired.

Evaluating expressions also follows precise rules to avoid some of the ambiguity found in ordinary arithmetic. For example, the value of

$$30/3*2$$

may be either 20 or 5, depending on which operator is applied first, / or *. The rules are

1   Expressions inside parentheses are evaluated first, starting with the innermost pair.

2   Expressions inside or outside parentheses are evaluated in order of the priority of the operator, that is, first the exponented constants or variables, then division or multiplication, and finally addition or subtraction. The hierarchy is then

$$** \text{ or}$$
$$* \text{ or } /$$
$$+ \text{ or } -$$

When priorities are equal, such as * or /, evaluate from left to right. Try, for example,

$$(4 - 3 \uparrow 2 * 2 / (5+1)) * 2$$

which should give you 2 as a result.

CALCULATION AND PROGRAM CONTROL

The LET statement is an arithmetic assignment statement, the simplest kind. As already shown, it takes the form

$$\text{ln LET } v = e$$

or

$$\text{ln } v = e$$

where v is any variable name, e is any arithmetic expression (including a constant), and = means "be assigned the value of" or "be replaced by." We can use BASIC as a kind of calculator because e can be any complex expression; for example,

$$\text{ln } Z = X**3+2X**X+1.4*X+3.9$$

will evaluate Z for any previously defined value of X.

The simplest *control* statement is the GO TO, an unconditional branch to the following line number; for example,

$$\text{ln GO TO ln}_1$$

It *controls* the program by altering the normal sequence of execution, in order of line number, forcing a branch to ln_1. GO TO can be used to program a *loop*, a repeating sequence of commands, which is what was done in our sample program. Unless the loop is to go on forever (or as long as power is up), it is necessary to include an escape statement within the loop, such as lines 50 and 70 in the example.

The IF THEN statements, lines 50 and 70, rely on something changing within the program so as to make them true or false. The something is the *relational operator* following IF, of the form

$$e_1 \text{ op } e_2$$

where e_1 and e_2 are any expressions and the op (operators) are

Operator	Meaning
$=$	Equal to
$<=$ or $=<$	Less than or equal to
$<$	Less than
$>$	Greater than
$>=$ or $=>$	Greater than or equal to
$<>$ or $><$	Not equal to

Thus $2*A >= 8$ is TRUE if the variable A takes on the value of 4 or more during the program, otherwise it is FALSE.

$$ln \text{ IF } e_1 \text{ op } e_2 \text{ THEN } ln_1$$

or

$$ln \text{ IF } e_1 \text{ op } e_2 \text{ GOTO } ln_1$$

Both have the same effect, a *conditional transfer of control* to statement ln_1 if and only if the relational statement e_1 op e_2 is TRUE. We have already seen how this works in the sample program. Another form of IF statement found in some small BASIC interpreters is

$$ln \text{ IF } e_1 \text{ op } e_2 \text{ LET } e_3 = e_4$$

or

$$ln \text{ IF } e_1 \text{ op } e_2 \text{ THEN } e_3 = e_4$$

This substitutes an arithmetic expression for the control statement; for example,

$$ln \text{ IF } a > B \text{ LET } X = 15$$

Certain larger BASIC computers allow even more complex IF statements, such as three-branch statements, but these are not discussed, as they are seldom available for microprocessors.

INPUT/OUTPUT

One of the beauties of BASIC, as far as the tyro programmer is concerned, is that there is no need to worry about formatting, or where and how the output is printed. In FORTRAN, for example, or even more so in COBOL, a good fraction of the programmer's effort is spent specifying the exact output format to follow. BASIC automatically gives a simple but usable output on the bare statement.

$$\text{ln PRINT } a_1, a_2, a_3, \ldots$$

where a_i is any item whose value is to be printed out. If the a_i are separated by commas, a nominal zone spacing (often about 13 spaces) is used to separate the items. They will be aligned across the page and in right-justified columns or, in floating-point, with decimal points aligned. If semicolons are used instead of commas, the items will be more densely packed, and printed with only enough space to be legible. The a_1 may include variables, in which case the current value is printed, or constants, or even expressions. Thus in the "calculator" mode we can write a statement such as

$$\text{ln PRINT } 1.45**2 - 3*(1.29 - 0.512)$$

and receive a printed result:

$$-.232$$

We can also PRINT what is called an alphanumeric *literal* or *string* of literals. A literal string is any character or character sequence (including blanks) enclosed in quotation marks, such as

```
10 PRINT
20 PRINT "THIS PROGRAM SEARCHES LISTS"
30 END
```

which will result in a blank line (the first PRINT) followed by

THIS PROGRAM SEARCHES LISTS

and a carriage return.

Input has been considered in our sample program only through the method of a DATA list. This is not the best way to introduce data because the program must be altered each time the list is changed. Data can also be entered from a keyboard (terminal) using the statement INPUT:

$$\ln \text{INPUT } v_1, v_2, \ldots$$

where v_1 is a list of variables.

The program will halt and usually print out a

$$?$$

which is followed by the operator entering a constant value from the keyboard. For example,

```
10 INPUT X
20 PRINT X + 2
30 END
```

will result in the output (assuming the operator enters the underlined number)

$$\frac{?\ 10}{12}$$

More than one constant can be entered after the question mark; these are separated by commas and terminated by a carriage return. Values are assigned to each of the variables in the list in sequence. Extra constants are ignored and, if not enough are supplied, another ? will be printed.

Some new BASIC interpreters allow INPUT to be used with quotes in a PRINT capacity also, thus saving program memory. For example,

$$\ln \text{INPUT ``ENTER VALUE FOR Y''; Y}$$

Many other variations of INPUT are found, including those allowing input from a data port.

FOR-TO-NEXT LOOPS

These constructs offer a method of program control that is more sophisticated than GOTO or IF-THEN statements, using the concept of repetition or looping. The FOR-TO-NEXT statement has three parts, stated or implied: a counter variable, an end test, and an increment. The general statement is

$$\text{ln FOR } v = e_1 \text{ TO } e_2 \text{ STEP } e_3$$

where v is the counter variable, e_1 is an expression which when evaluated becomes the initial value of v, e_2 is the final value of v, and e_3 is the increment added to v at each repetition. (If STEP is omitted, e_3 is assumed to be 1.)

A block of statements that are to be repeated follow the FOR line. After the end of the block is the NEXT statement

$$\text{ln NEXT } v$$

where v is the same variable chosen as a counter.

As an example, consider the following program segment:

```
10  FOR X = 1 TO 9 STEP 2
20  Y = X*2
30  PRINT Y;
40  NEXT X
50  . . .
```

This results in the printout

$$2 \quad 6 \quad 10 \quad 14 \quad 18$$

The block of statements 20, 30 is executed first for $X = 1$, then for $X = 1 + 2 = 3$, then for $X = 5$, and so forth, adding the STEP value 2 to X each time. At each block repetition the NEXT statement returns control to line 10 and the counter X is incremented again by STEP. The last repetition occurs when $X = 9$. Another increment would exceed the upper limit TO 9, and the control of the program would continue with line 50, the statement following the NEXT X of line 40.

In the event that STEP is omitted or not supported by the interpreter or compiler, BASIC assumes that the value of the increment is 1. The above program segment without STEP will print

$$2 \quad 4 \quad 6 \quad 8 \ldots 18$$

When STEP is permitted, the increment value may be negative or even a floating point value such as 0.5.

EXAMPLE OF A BASIC PROGRAM

If our BASIC supports all the variations described above, the list searching program could be rewritten in a more elegant form (Figure 4-3). Using the FOR-NEXT statement block (60 to 90) saves one line over the original program's IF statement block (50 to 90). In addition, the program is much more flexible, as the list length and search key name are keyboard inputs and can be changed on each run without altering the program. Furthermore, the use of literal strings permits the names to be written out in plain English rather than a code such as ASCII.

BASIC VARIATIONS

Ongoing programs exist to standardize BASIC by the National Bureau of Standards and the American National Standards Institute (ANSI). Most of the features mentioned here are supported by the ANSI standard. There are other BASIC features, both ANSI and non-standard, which are found in one or another, but not in all interpreters and compilers. Microprocessor BASICs, especially those using 4K or less of memory, naturally have the fewest features and may be confined to 1-byte integers (0 to 255). Some of the most basic features not covered here are

ATN (n): returns arctangent (radian value).

SIN (n), COS (n), TAN (n): trigonometric functions.

LOG (n) and CLOG (n): natural and common logarithms.

SQR: square.

DIM (n, m): a valuable method of reserving space to store and retrieve lists of elements as arrays or matrices (two-dimensional arrays).

ELSE: alternate branch to an IF statement.

ON-GO TO: A three-way branch statement.

```
  1   REM ENTER NAME LIST ON DATA LINE 10

 10   DATA "JONES", "SMITH", "BROWN", ... "ABLE", ...

 20   PRINT "ENTER NUMBER OF NAMES IN LIST"

 30   INPUT N

 40   PRINT "ENTER NAME OF KEY"

 50   INPUT X$

 60   FOR J = 1 TO N

 70   READ K$

 80   IF K$ = X$ GOTO 110

 90   NEXT J

100   PRINT "LIST DOES NOT CONTAIN "; X$

105   GOTO 120

110   PRINT X$; "IS NUMBER "; J; " IN LIST"

120   END
```

```
Example of Program Use:


ENTER NUMBER OF NAMES IN LIST
? 10
ENTER NAME OF KEY
? BROWN
BROWN IS NUMBER 3 IN LIST
```

Figure 4–3 List searching program.

FN: allows a user-defined function such as an expression using builtin functions.
GO SUB: branch to a subroutine. RETURN brings control back to the main program.

These are supported by most BASIC compilers.

Any BASIC interpreter or compiler is furnished with documentation which is the final authority for that version of the language. A good reference to the many variants available is *The BASIC Handbook* by David Lien.[2]

REFERENCES

1   Knuth, D. E., "Algorithms," *Scientific American*, **236**, 63–80 (April 1977).
2   Lien, D. L., *The BASIC Handbook*, San Diego: Compusoft (1978).
3   *Mini-Micro Systems*, **13**, 105 (June 1980).

5

Other High Level Languages

Useful and universal as BASIC is, it would not be correct to leave the impression that it is the only high level language (HLL) available for microprocessor use, nor necessarily the best. Micro*computers*, which now include 16-bit machines equipped with millions of bytes of floppy disk memory, can use almost any HLL, including such specialized members as COBOL (Common Business Oriented Language) and APL, an interactive scientific language particularly suitable for logical functions. But such large microcomputers are nearly indistinguishable from the minicomputers with which they compete. We are concerned here primarily with micro*processor* product applications other than general computing where mass memory peripherals may not be permissible from a cost standpoint and minimum on-board memory usage is desirable. Thus we want to be able to use HLL for economy and convenience in program development, and on occasion to take advantage of the microprocessor's flexible potential through user programmability. Pre-programmed instruments can be *configured*, that is, portions of the program may be selected through such means as special-purpose keyboards, thumbwheel switches, and the like, but an HLL such as BASIC, which can be readily understood and quickly learned (as distinguished from assembly languages), is the only practical way to achieve user programmability.

The effectiveness of HLLs in reducing programming cost, specifically in the development of large programs, is undeniable. A typical example cited by *Mini-Micro Systems*[1] shows that 16,000 lines of assembly code can take three programmers 16 months at a cost of $240,000 ($15 per line), while the same program can be written in 8000 lines of an HLL in 8 months at a cost of $120,000. However, the penalty is loss of code compactness and efficiency, since the HLL of the example requires one-third more storage—64K bytes of memory compared to 48K for assembly language. Krieger and Planger[2] have estimated that a good assembly programmer can take 15 to 30% off of a good compiler by using C code, an HLL developed by Bell Laboratories and now in general use. Still, they conclude that HLL usage is adequately justified in lower programming costs. Furthermore, optimized compilers are becoming available which are 90% efficient in terms of speed and space compared to very good assembly programmers. Obviously, however, assembly programming is best for very small programs such as those used in toys.

ALTERNATIVES TO BASIC

BASIC is a poor tool for real-time control because it is slow. Input and output routines are awkward, and it is difficult to manipulate bits. In contrast to newer languages, it is not inherently structured. Programming several concurrent tasks or processes by different programmers working independently is rendered nearly impossible.[3] Reliance on the GOTO construct makes programs difficult to trace and debug.

FORTRAN

FORTRAN (*For*mula *Tran*slation) is possibly the next best known and most widely used HLL and is considered to be richer and more powerful than BASIC. Actually, FORTRAN is considerably older (having been developed in 1957 for the IBM-704 computer about 10 years before BASIC's appearance at Dartmouth), but it has undergone a number of revisions, of which FORTRAN IV and FORTRAN 77 are currently the most used.[4] Like BASIC, FORTRAN is a set of statements used to solve a problem, but rather than being interpreted statement by statement, it is compiled into machine language. Constants are similar to BASIC, but a distinction is made in naming integer and floating point variables. Subscripted variables (arrays) are supported, as are the five arithmetic operators and standard functions such as SIN, TAN, and LOG, which can be used in assignment statements ($a = e$, where e is an expression). Control statements include GOTO and the powerful DO, which repeats a block of statements within a specified control range much like BASIC's FOR-TO-STEP statement.

FORTRAN subroutine variables can be declared locally or in a COMMON area of memory where they are *global*, that is, used for both main and subprograms. FORTRAN input and output are more highly developed than in BASIC, and there is much flexibility in output format.

Despite its advantage of greater capability, FORTRAN is not frequently resident in microprocessors, since it requires a large compiler and usually a disk storage system. It is widely used in minicomputer control systems, including process control and on military applications, where the DOD (Department of Defense) version (FORTRAN 77) has been mandated. Programs in FORTRAN can be *cross-compiled*, that is, developed on another computer or on a microprocessor development system such as those furnished by National Semiconductor, Zilog, and Texas Instruments, and the object code can be installed in a specific microprocessor, usually in ROM or PROM.

PL/1 AND DERIVATIVES

Although it has the advantage of being familiar to many engineers, FORTRAN suffers from some of the same faults as BASIC and has the added burden of the large compiler. A better candidate is PL/1 in one of its many versions specifically designed for microprocessor use. PL/1 is a structured language originally developed by IBM. Although the GOTO is permitted, it is not necessary, since many other constructs (IF-THEN-ELSE, DO WHILE, DO CASE, which we examine later in this chapter) do the same job. Eliminating GOTO allows the program to flow down the page and be more easily traced.

PL/1 anticipates many of the features of Pascal, a language that we discuss at more length. Programs are constructed in blocks (called procedures), which allows for easy programming of concurrent processes. Promoting this kind of teamwork is the concept of confining variables to a specific procedure; thus two or more persons can program different procedures without prior agreement on the assignment of variable names. Storage is normally allotted to variables on entry into the procedure in which the variable is defined. However, variations are possible, such as explicit allocation by the programmer through statements.

PL/M is the microprocessor version of PL/1, and PL/M-80 was the first application developed for the Intel 8080 and 8085 microprocessors, 8-bit CPUs.[5] It is used as a resident compiler. A more modern version is being developed for the 8086, known as PL/M-86. Both PL/Ms are block structured and support the extended IF-type conditional instructions of PL/1, facilitating the constructing of control algorithms. Another PL/1 version has been developed by Rockwell International for the 6502 microprocessors; this is called PL/65. It is available as a resident compiler or can run on the DEC PDP-11 minicomputer as a cross-compiler. A diskette (floppy disk) is a necessary adjunct for the development system, which includes text editor, assembler, and debug features.

MPL, another PL/1-like HLL, was available for the Motorola 6800 microprocessors but has been replaced in their development system by Pascal. Zilog's PLZ/SYS, developed for the Z-80 family, utilizes features of both the PL/1 and Pascal languages, and is also block structured. Both compilers and interpreters have been written for this HLL.

FORTH

Forth, a highly sophisticated HLL derived from the MIT-developed STOIC, is much less well known to engineers in general but highly regarded by a coterie of programming professionals. It is worthy of special note from several points of view, and many reports claim great programming efficiency for Forth as compared to FORTRAN. Often tasks that required several programmer-months to implement in Forth are contrasted with estimates of several programmer-years using FORTRAN. While Forth is viewed as an HLL, it keeps the programmer closer to the machine level of the processor than is the case for other languages. This characteristic is partly responsible for its efficiency. The language is "stack oriented," and the programmer must be constantly aware of the content and order of the stack. This orientation in turn forces a certain amount of structure on the programmer.

A Forth program appears at first glance to be an assembly language program because it is not built up with a core of natural language words as is the case in BASIC and FORTRAN. However, it does have sophisticated operations, and the programs are readily followed by the programmer who has become familiar with Forth. Its advantages include running speed (claimed to be 10 times faster than BASIC), suitability to multitask jobs such as process control, lower memory requirements than other HLLs or even assembly programs, adaptability to small memories and short word length, and extreme flexibility. Forth can do anything that can be done in assembly language, including such "illogical" operations as adding an integer to a boolean variable. As a result it can be dangerous to use for those less than expert.

The basic concept of the language is what is called indirect-threaded coding. The language is organized as a dictionary with no set number of operations. The programmer defines and saves procedures called *words*, which are denoted to the compiler by " . . . " or ": . . . ". These procedures are then called by using the defined word. Forth uses pushdown stacks (last-in first-out, LIFO), and operates in accordance with reverse Polish notation much like Hewlett-Packard hand calculators. Each operator acts directly on the preceding entity on the stack so that no parentheses are needed. For example, the normal arithmetic expression

$$12 * 2400/45$$

would be rendered in Forth (reverse Polish notation) as

$$12 \ 2400 * 45 \ /$$

meaning that 12 on top of the stack is pushed down by 2400, then the top two are multiplied by the operator *, the product is pushed down by 45, and again the top two operated on by the divide symbol /.

The programmer creates new words for the dictionary by combining defined words from a core of 100 in the operating system and those new words he has already defined. Such combined words act as functions or procedures, and eliminate the need to jump to subroutines and return. This accounts for some of the speed of Forth (about 75% of the speed of assembly language). Each complex word so defined becomes a string of addresses threading their way through the dictionary. For example, the definition for APPLE may be[6]

$$: \text{APPLE MEDIUM SIZE ROUND RED FRUIT ;}$$

where each of the defining words (e.g., MEDIUM) have been themselves defined earlier and given an address in the dictionary.

A particular microprocessor version, microFORTH, utilizes 6K of disk for the compiler and editor, and a 512-byte run-time support nucleus that is resident on the microprocessor board. A number of Forth versions are available for the 8080, 8085, Z-80, LSI-11, RCA-1802, TI 9900, and Motorola 6800. Apart from commercial groups, the language is supported by the FORTH Interest Group of San Carlos, California. Some idea of the advantage over FORTRAN can be obtained from the following example, representing an actual case history.[7]

The application included setup and control of an instrument, real-time data acquisition, real-time graphics display, third-order function least squares fitting, Fourier analysis, and servicing of panel control function buttons. This program was estimated for FORTRAN as requiring 3 programmer-years and 32K words of computer memory. Use of Forth resulted in an 8K word memory implementation with 1 programmer-year of programming.

C-CODE

C, a development of the Bell System, is larger and more powerful than most HLLs, and was once exclusively applied to the Bell Labs one-chip CMOS MAC-4 microcomputer. Despite the use of more operator/operand combinations than Pascal, for example, C-code can be compiled into a memory space no worse than 10 to 30% larger than that for the best assembly language. Its greatest disadvantage is the large compiler size—at least 60K bytes for an 8080 or Z-80 target.

C was originated by D. M. Ritchie at Bell Laboratories in the early 1970s, and was seldom used outside this activity due to its high licensing fee. In recent years a commercial firm, Whitesmiths, Ltd.,[8] has developed a compiler suitable for the 8080, Z-80, and LSI-11 which is available at competitive rates.

Since a full discussion of C is beyond the scope of this chapter, the reader is referred to Ritchie's book[9] and articles discussing its strengths and weaknesses.[10]

PASCAL

Pascal is a highly structured language that has rapidly become one of the most highly valued HLLs in both academic and industrial circles. It was originally developed in 1968 by Niklaus Wirth in Zurich as a teaching tool and an aid to writing easily understood and logical programs, but was developed further at the University of California—San Diego by K. Jensen and K. Bowles to the point where it became suitable for microprocessor applications.[11] Pascal has most of the advantages sought in an HLL: block structure, strong typing and control of variables, concurrent program support, and a sparse but efficient set of operators, functions, statements, procedures, and types that will support the most sophisticated control system programs. Pascal is a derivative of ALGOL, an early European rival of FORTRAN, and has been also called "PL/1 done right."[12]

Although Pascal uses a fairly large compiler (20K for the LSI-11), it has become practical for microprocessors because of the development of an intermediate or P-code, which is transformed by a small resident interpreter into the machine language. P-Code interpreters are available for the 8080, Z-80, 6800, 9900, and other target microprocessors. Western Digital has in addition developed a 16-bit microprocessor, the WD/90, that executes directly the instructions of P-code, making an interpreter unnecessary.[13] Thus there are several ways in which Pascal can be implemented, by compiling to P-code and interpreting that code, by cross-compiling to the native machine language of the processor, or by direct use of P-code after compiling from Pascal.

Use of P-code has its disadvantages, of course. Any change of the program must be recompiled. To put a Pascal compiler in an operating system such as the Apple III (6502 microprocessor), 14K of memory is needed (an 8K ROM is available[14] for the 6800 and 6809 but additional room is needed for a program). Pascal has also been criticized on other, more fundamental grounds, such as lack of dynamic arrays (subscripted variable size must be declared at the start of the program), and the difficulty in handling random access files. The best way to demonstrate its advantage is by actual use and example.

PASCAL EXAMPLE

We could demonstrate the features of the Pascal language by continuing with the example of the last chapter, but it would be inappropriate on several counts. For one, the program is not particularly well suited to display Pascal's features, which include structure, clearly indicating the different functions of the program; modularity or "building-block" program construction; and strong typing, rigidly defining the exact nature of permissible variations and constants. By means of these language features, Pascal programs are constrained to be written unambiguously, are easy to understand, and have builtin precautions against errors. It is clear that programs will be more free of logical errors if they are put together from smaller and better defined modules. Pascal helps prevent data input errors by requiring all variable types to be defined (e.g., ASCII character or integer or real number), and even allows the programmer to define his own data types. It is possible to define, for example, a certain type of variable to be the integers 0 to 9 or real numbers less than 100.0, or even the days of the week. Any misplaced data attempting to enter that part of the program would be immediately spotted and declared illegal by Pascal. On the other hand BASIC does not make these fine distinctions, so that an integer, for instance, can be entered in place of a real number and run in most cases.

Another reason for choosing a new example is that one weakness of Pascal is the inability to read strings of characters easily, since the standard procedure "read" is designed to accept only one character at a time, unlike BASIC's INPUT command. The read procedure can be made to accept a string, but only by entering characters one at a time into an array or indexed list of characters (see BASIC's DIM command). This makes the program too complicated for a beginning example.

Let us assume that we want to perform a simple arithmetic calculation, adding two real numbers ("real" means the same as floating point and is distinguished from "integer"). Also, we want to set off the calculation by printing it between two dashed lines. The real numbers are to be entered from a terminal (keyboard) and the program is to continue asking for more input until we enter "0.0" into the terminal.

The program is concerned with the manipulation of different kinds of data (characters such as dashes and numerical variables), and can logically be separated into different tasks or segments and into a hierarchy of subtasks. This can be seen in Figure 5-1.

PROGRAM CONSTRUCTION

There are three major parts to this program. In the beginning Pascal requires us to define the data type of each variable before it is used. It is also considered good practice to define constants (such as the length of the dashed line) rather than use them as literals in the program body. This promotes portability—the ability to move the program to a different terminal or computer—one of the major advantages of an HLL. As in many other HLLs, we can easily change the line length if it was defined in the initial declaration; otherwise it might have to be changed in several places (or forgotten in one).

Next, we want to define any special "procedures," such as the method of creating or drawing the dashed line, or any other quirks of coding routine that are repetitive and perhaps unique to this program. A Pascal PROCEDURE is very like a subroutine in BASIC (GOSUB), but must be defined before use in the main program.

A procedure is itself structured like a program. Constants and variables can be defined for exclusive use within the procedure. The memory space they occupy is then given up and can be reused (overwritten) by other coding after exiting from the procedure. Alternately, the procedure may use global variables that were defined ahead of the procedure, but the converse is not true. This fine control over the span of existence of variables and constants is one of the strong points of Pascal.

Finally, after defining the tools to be used, we can enter the main body of the program. The structure of the main program can then be broad and top-down, since the details are defined in the procedures and can be invoked by merely naming them.

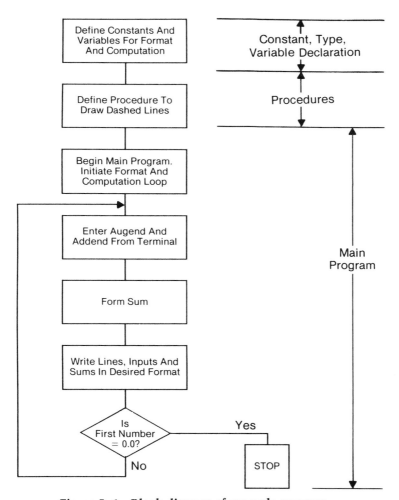

Figure 5–1 Block diagram of example program.

Figure 5-1 shows the operations that we wish to perform in the example program and how they are divided by a Pascal implementation. The sections are typical but not mandatory in all Pascal programs. This can be shown more clearly by means of *syntax* diagrams, such as Figure 5-2, which describe the mandatory structure of any Pascal program. For example, in Figure 5-2A it is seen that a program need only consist of a heading and a block and is ended by a period. (Spaces, lines, and indentations are disregarded by the Pascal compiler but are important to human understanding, so should always be present.)

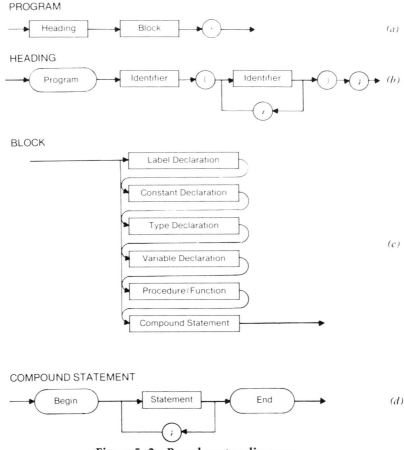

Figure 5–2 Pascal syntax diagrams.

The Pascal program heading must always begin with the word PROGRAM; this is a *reserved word* in the language, must always be used as in the syntax diagram (Figure 5-2B) and is capitalized here for clarity. PROGRAM must be followed by an *identifier* which names the program. Identifiers are another strong point of Pascal; they are descriptive names assigned by the programmer to be used for constants, types, variables, procedures, and functions. An identifier consists of a letter followed by any combination of letters and digits desired by the programmer. Standard Pascal only distinguishes the first eight characters of the identifiers; thus the variables *numberofdesks* and *numberofpupils* could not be separated because the first eight letters are the same, but *desknumber* and *pupilnumber* would be acceptable. Longer and more descriptive variable names are, of course, a better interface to the programmer.

Following the program name identifier are additional identifiers representing *files* of data. Since most programs request input data and output data to some peripheral like a CRT screen or printer, the standard file names (input, output) are normally found in this place. Note that they are enclosed in parentheses and separated by a comma. If the read or write procedures are not used, input or output files may be omitted (except that in some Pascal compilers output must always be present to allow for error messages). For example, we could write a perfectly valid Pascal program as follows:

```
PROGRAM addones (output);
BEGIN
     write (1 + 1)
END.
```

This program would print the value 2 on a terminal. Because it could not do anything else, it would not be very useful. A much better program would define variables, use the read procedure to input them, and then perform the desired arithmetic and output.

Other kinds of files can be defined and used, but in contrast to input and output they must be declared in the variable declaration section, as well as the program heading. For example, we can write the output of a program to a file to be stored on disk and used in another program.

The heading must be terminated by a semicolon.

BLOCKS

The *block* is the fundamental unit of a Pascal program. The block describes the data (declarations), as well as the action to be taken (statements). Figure 5-2C shows only the block options and order in which they must appear, if used. It does not show the punctuation (delimiter) symbols that are essential to the program.

The one part of the block that is mandatory is the compound statement. The statement is the action part, like write ( ) in the earlier example. "Compound" refers to the words BEGIN and END, which are reserved words and act in the same way as arithmetic parentheses. Any number of statements can be put between BEGIN and END; all but the last must be separated by the semicolon (;). The statement before END need not be followed by a semicolon because the END itself acts as a delimiter. If one is put in, we have a "null statement," one that does nothing. Actually, since a null statement takes up time, it can be used as a time delay if we know how long the CPU takes to process it.

A statement may be a compound statement. A compound statement is a sequence of simple or compound statements. That is, statements can be *recursive* and therefore nested at different levels. This is a very useful feature.

There are seven different kinds of statements in standard Pascal, some of which are similar to those encountered in BASIC. These are IF-THEN-ELSE, REPEAT-UNTIL, WHILE-DO, FOR-TO (or DOWN-TO), CASE, WITH, and GOTO. These are in addition to the assignment statement and procedure calls, including read and write statements. Rather than describe all of these we return to the program diagrammed in Figure 5-1 and show the more common features of the language by example.

TOP-DOWN VIEW OF PROGRAM

Figure 5-3 is the actual program written in Electro Scientific Industries (ESI) Pascal.[15] Line 10 is the program heading as described above. (Line numbers are used for the convenience of the editor program and are included here for identification.) The program identifier is the name "addlines" and the files are input, output. The next six lines are comment and spacing for legibility. Comments in the ESI language are set off by the symbols /* and */. Full comments (on separate lines or on program lines) are highly recommended to explain and clarify the less obvious parts of the program and to encourage the discipline of good documentation.

Following the top-down philosphy, the main program is sketched first. This part specifies what the program is to perform and in what sequence, in terms of variables and procedures that are either standard or are defined in other parts of the program. In actually developing such a program, we work back and forth, alternating between the main program and procedures until each is adjusted to accomplish the desired effects.

The main program starts with the highest level (leftmost) BEGIN following the sections labeled PROCEDURE. The first action is to prepare a dashed line of specified length to be used repetitively in the format. This is done by means of a procedure we call "filline" (line 390). Filline does not actually draw a line but merely specifies what will be

```
10PROGRAM addlines (input,output);
20
30/* This prosram formats an addition procedure settins off the addends
40and the sum by means of dashed lines.  Procedure filline fills a
50character array with dashes only once in the prosram while procedure
60drawline actually writes the dashed line whenever it is called.*/
70
80CONST
90     max=70;
100
110VAR
120     line: ARRAY[1..max] OF char;
130     i: integer;
140     sum, firstnum, secnum:real;
150
160/* line and i are both global variables so they may be called by both
170procedures */
180
190PROCEDURE filline;
200
210     CONST
220         dash='-';
230
240     BEGIN
250        FOR i := 1 TO max DO
260            line[i] := dash
270     END; /*end of filline*/
280
290PROCEDURE drawline;
300
310     BEGIN
320        FOR i:= 1 TO max DO
330            write(line[i]:1);
340        writeln
350     END; /*end of drawline*/
360
370
380BEGIN /*main prosram*/
390     filline;
400     firstnum := 1.0;
410     WHILE firstnum > 0.0 DO
420        BEGIN
430            writeln('Enter 2 real numbers; 0.0 to stop');
440            read(firstnum,secnum);
450            sum := firstnum+secnum;
460            drawline;
470            writeln(' ':10,'FIRST NUMBER :',firstnum);
480            writeln;
490            writeln(' ':10,'SECOND NUMBER:',secnum);
500            writeln;
510            writeln;(' ':10,'SUM',' ':10,':',sum);
520            writeln;
530            drawline
540        END/*end of WHILE*/
550END./*end of addlines*/
```

Figure 5–3   Pascal program "addlines."

117

drawn. The next activity is to introduce data in the form of the two numbers to be added, which we call "firstnum" and "secnum." These are input from the terminal by the user. The program is to run over and over until the user is finished with it; this is signified by putting in the real number 0.0 at the terminal. One Pascal method of accomplishing this is the WHILE statement

410 WHILE firstnum > 0.0 DO
(compound statement)

This means that the statements following WHILE will be repeated over and over as long as the conditional expression

firstnum > 0.0

is true at the beginning of the loop. To be sure that it will run at least once, we must set the value of firstrun to 1.0 (any defined number greater than zero will do) by means of the *assignment* statement before entering the WHILE:

400 firstnum: = 1.0;

After it has been established that the WHILE statement will run, the first action of its compound statement (the second level BEGIN) is to write a message to the user requesting entry of data from the terminal. The *writeln* statement is a form of write and acts by printing out the literal characters between single quotes, after which it gives a carriage return and begins a new line. Because this is not the last statement in the WHILE, it must be followed by a semicolon to separate it from the next statement:

read (firstnum, secnum);

Note that the read statement can request multiple inputs by naming more than one variable to be assigned.

This statement reads the two real numbers (separated by a comma) that the user types into the terminal. If anything other than real numbers are entered, an error message is returned. If the user wants to terminate the WHILE, 0.0 is entered as the first number.

Having acquired the data, the program will add the two numbers in order to write them later. (Note that BASIC could omit this step, as the value of the expression

```
Enter 2 real numbers; 0.0 to stop
2.,4.
....... ...... ...... ...... ...... ...... ......

          FIRST NUMBER  :  2.000000E+00

          SECOND NUMBER:  4.000000E+00

          SUM           :  6.000000E+00


...... ...... ...... ...... ...... ...... ......
Enter 2 real numbers; 0.0 to stop
222.,444.
....... ...... ...... ...... ...... ...... ......

          FIRST NUMBER  :  2.220000E+02

          SECOND NUMBER:  4.440000E+02

          SUM           :  6.660000E+02


...... ...... ...... ...... ...... ...... ......
Enter 2 real numbers; 0.0 to stop
3.14596, 2.7184
....... ...... ...... ...... ...... ...... ......

          FIRST NUMBER  :  3.141596E+00

          SECOND NUMBER:  2.718400E+00

          SUM           :  5.859996E+00


...... ...... ...... ...... ...... ...... ......
Enter 2 real numbers; 0.0 to stop
0.0,0.0
....... ...... ...... ...... ...... ...... ......

          FIRST NUMBER  :  0.000000E+00

          SECOND NUMBER:  0.000000E+00

          SUM           :  0.000000E+00


...... ...... ...... ...... ...... ...... ......
```

Figure 5–4 Output of Pascal program "addlines."

firstnum + secnum

could be assigned to "sum" in BASIC's write statement, but this is not so in Pascal.)

The remainder of the program is concerned only with the format of the printed output. The statement

drawline;

is a call to the procedure of that name, just as "filline" called its procedure. In this case "drawline;" actually prints the line formatted by filline on the terminal directly under the user's input (see Figure 5-4). Note that we can draw this line anyplace in the format merely by calling the procedure name, but that it is only necessary to set it up with "filline" once.

The writeln statements on lines 470, 490, and 510 print multiple outputs on the same line; formats are separated by commas. The statement

$$\text{writeln } (1:n);$$

prints the literal right-justified in a field of width n. Since in line 470 the literal is a blank, the effect is to leave 10 spaces blank. The second action of line 470 is to print the literal string, and thirdly the value of the variable firstnum. Note that since no field width is given in this last statement, a default value will be chosen (see Figure 5-4).

Having printed the output in the desired format (including drawing a second line by means of the "drawline" statement on line 530), what does the program do? It depends on the last value of firstnum read at the terminal. The control of the program returns to WHILE, and the expression is evaluated again. If firstrun was evaluated as 0.0 in the previous cycle, that is all—the WHILE terminates. Note, however, that this reading 0.0 did not prevent the previous cycle from completing; that is, 0.0 was read and printed out because WHILE only evaluates at the *beginning* of the cycle, not during its progress.

The WHILE statement is completed with an END (there must always be an END to match each BEGIN). Therefore there must also be another END to go with the BEGIN of the entire main program block. That END is terminated with a period, which completes the program. To distinguish between ENDs and promote program legibility, it is good practice to identify them with a brief comment.

While we have completed an overview of the program, in true top-down fashion, we have left a lot of important details to be cleared up. How do we declare the types, variables, and constants? How are the procedures written? To answer these questions we must enter into the "bottom-up" mode of program design.

DECLARATIONS

The first declaration part is for constants. This must begin with the reserved word CONST followed by declarations of the form identifier = constant;

The equals sign (=) does the assignment, and each declaration must be terminated by the semicolon. A constant may be any literal, real, integer, or character, but characters must be enclosed in single quotes; for example,

ch = 'X';
null = ' '; /* a blank character */
today = 'TG its Friday'; /* a string */

A constant may also be declared in terms of a previously defined constant identifier:

max = 1000000;
min = − max;

The next requirement is to declare variables, using the reserved word VAR. On line 130 we define the identifier i as an integer, using the colon:

i: integer;

and on one line (140) declare the three variable names sum, firstnum, and secnum as type real. These are simple standard types; the other standard types include *char* (single ASCII characters) and *boolean*, which has only the values true or false. Note that a real number (literal) must start with a digit and follow the decimal point (if used) with a digit; for example, 1 or 1.0 is allowed, but 1. is not.

The variable line on 120 requires more explanation because it is actually a shorthand declaration of both a variable and a type. The type is a complex one called a *structured* type, because it consists of more than one component. An array is merely an ordered collection of variables, all of the same *base* type. In the case of "line" the base type is character. Each variable in the array is indexed. The index type in this case consists of the integers 1 to max where is the constant 70, and the succession 1 to 70 is symbolized by the two dots. However, the index could be any *scalar* simple type. A scalar type is an ordered group, such as integer, or a *subrange* of integers that could be declared in a type declaration (before VAR), as in

TYPE
subscript = 1 . . 70;
letter = 'a' . . 'z';

where each member of the group can be said to be greater or less than another (2 is greater than 1, 'b' is greater than 'a'). Boolean type is also scalar, since implicitly (from the type declaration) false comes before true (false < true). However, a real type is *not* scalar and cannot be used in an array index.

A scalar type can be defined in a completely arbitrary way such as

TYPE
    workday = (monday, tuesday, wednesday, thursday, friday);

where the order is established by the declaration (tuesday, monday).

Although the index of the array must be scalar, the base can be of any type, including real, and importantly, can be an array itself. An array with an array for a base type is an *array of arrays* or a matrix. It can be thought of as a two-dimensional array of rows and columns. This array multidimensionality can be carried on recursively to dimensions higher than two, depending on the compiler.

An array can be assigned the value of another array of the same type by a simple assignment statement. Alternately, the *components* of the array may be assigned values by the same kind of statement.

To return to our program, the variable "line" is declared to be of the type ARRAY, and consists of characters distinguished by the integers 1 to 70. The components can be indicated individually by the format

line [i]

where i is one of the index integers.

Note that we have accomplished two things in this declaration: we have defined a variable "line" and also a specific type of ARRAY. This could have been done another way by declaring the type first and then the variable. In fact, this is the more standard way to do the job and may be somewhat clearer. For example, we declare

TYPE
    subscript = 1 .. max
    line   = ARRAY (subscript) OF char

VAR
    dashes, dots: line

In this case we first declared the scalar type "subscript" (a subrange of integer) and then used it as the index of the ARRAY type "line", which is of base type char; "line" is now a type, not a variable. We can now declare one or more variables, each of the type "line". This is therefore the most flexible method, since we can now have a line of dots and one of dashes, or any other combination that strikes our fancy, though, of course, it uses more source codes.

PROCEDURES

A procedure, as we have said earlier, is similar to a subroutine in BASIC or FORTRAN, and is much like a small program in itself. A program within a program infers hierarchal structure, and this is an apt description of a procedure.

As does the program, the procedure heading begins with a reserved word, PROCEDURE, and its identifier, for example, "filline" (line 190). The identifier is the means of calling the procedure, as we saw in the discussion of the main program block. The heading may also contain *formal parameters*, which are very important entities in some procedures. Simply, parameters are variables of two types. A *value parameter* is a means of transferring the value of a variable from the main program to the procedure. For example, if we had declared the parameter ch of type char in the procedure heading

PROCEDURE filline (ch:char);

and in the main program called filline by

filline (letter);

where letter was also a character variable, the procedure call would implicitly have made the assignment

ch: = letter;

If the value of the letter were 'y' at that point in the main program, that value would be transferred to the procedure. However, the value of the letter remains the same regardless of what is done to ch by the procedure. The other type of formal parameter is a VAR or *variable parameter*, declared by

PROCEDURE filline (VAR ch:char);

Now, if in the main program we call

filline (letter);

the variables "letter" and "ch" become synonymous. If "letter" enters "filline" with the value 'y' and is changed to 'z' by the procedure, its value in the main program becomes 'z' on return from the procedure.

The simple examples we have chosen do not require this powerful tool. However, procedures are also allowed to declare *local variables* and constants in the same way as programs. The constant "dash" in filline has the value '−' only in the procedure. If it were called anyplace else, such as in the drawline or the main program, it would have no meaning and would return an error. It is good practice to use local variables and constants because the space they occupy is given up as soon as the procedure is left.

On the contrary the *global variables* and constants that were declared in the main program, such as i, line and max, do retain their identity and can be used anywhere in the procedures or main program. Therefore another way of transferring values from procedures to the main program is to use global variables, such as line.

Procedure filline is quite simple. Its purpose is to assign the value of the constant "dash" to each component of the array line up to a maximimum of 70 components. In other words, line becomes an array of 70 '−' characters. The method of doing this is the FOR-TO statement. This is essentially the same as the FOR statement in BASIC or FORTRAN. Note that we could also have used the WHILE term by adding the statement

$$i: = i + 1;$$

but the FOR is preferred because it is easier to read the limits.

The procedure drawline is similar in structure to filline in that it also uses a FOR statement; however, it does not require any local variables. The variable i is global, and line is defined before drawline is called. Note that if the main program were to call drawline before filline, the value of the variable line would be indeterminate, hence this would be an execution error. It might be better program design to *nest* procedure filline within procedure drawline to ensure against this error. Nesting is allowed in Pascal procedures as well as in compound statements. For example, this program could look like the following (in outline):

Program addlines (   );
CONST

```
. . .
VAR
. . .
PROCEDURE drawline;
   PROCEDURE filline;
      CONST
         dash = '-';
      BEGIN
         . . .
      END; /* end of filline */
   BEGIN /* procedure drawline */
   filline;
      . . .
   END; /* end of drawline */
BEGIN /* main program */
```

OTHER STATEMENT TYPES

We have examined the WHILE and FOR statements briefly. Another statement similar to WHILE is the REPEAT. This is of the form

```
REPEAT
   statements
UNTIL condition
```

The condition is a boolean expression as before, and the statements enclosed are repeated until the value of condition is FALSE. The major difference between REPEAT and WHILE is that the condition of RE-PEAT is evaluated after the statement (end of the loop) instead of at the beginning. In both, the statements must contain something that will change the value of conditions or the loops will not terminate.

Another powerful statement is IF-THEN-ELSE, which is similar to the IF statement in BASIC. The form is

```
IF boolean expression
THEN   statement
ELSE   statement
```

The expression (condition) is evaluated and, if true, the THEN statement is executed. If not, the alternative following ELSE is executed. ELSE may be omitted, in which case nothing is done if the boolean expression is false; the program goes to the next statement following the IF-THEN.

The statements within IF may be compound and may be other IF statements; that is, IFs may be nested. This is called a *compound IF statement*, and the form is

IF condition I
  THEN statement I
  ELSE
    IF condition 2
      THEN statement 2
      ELSE statement 3
      or
IF alpha
  THEN
    IF beta
      THEN gamma
      ELSE delta
  ELSE epsilon

where alpha, beta, . . . , epsilon are conditions or statements. Other forms may be contrived by the programmer.

GOTO and CASE

GOTO should be mentioned, as it is present also in BASIC, but Pascal programs can be written without it, and in fact are better structured if it is not used. GOTO is a direct transfer of control to the statement indicated by the LABEL that can optionally be declared (see BLOCK syntax, Figure −2e). The GOTO can be used to jump out of a loop or to jump out of an error sequence, but cannot be used to jump *into* a loop or procedure. That is, you can go up a level with GOTO but not into a lower level (nest).

CASE is a much more elegant form of statement that is unique to Pascal. It is like IF but allows for multiple action, depending on the value of a scalar or subrange expression called a *case selector*. These selectors can be integers or scalar type declared by the user, such as

school type = (elementary, junior, senior, college);

or whatever the programmer desires. Say that we wish to convert decimal numbers to hexadecimal by writing the integers 10, 11, . . . , 15 as A, B, . . . , F. The following CASE statement will do this:

```
CASE digit OF
    10:         write      ('A' : 1);
    11:         write      ('B' : 1);
    12:         write      ('C' : 1);
    13:         write      ('D' : 1);
    14:         write      ('E' : 1);
    15:         write      ('F' : 1);
    ELSE        write      (digit)
END /* CASE digit */
```

(Note that all compilers do not allow ELSE in the CASE statement.)

The CASE selectors are the integers 10 through 15. Whenever the variable digit has the value of any of the selector integers, the corresponding letter is written; for example, CASE 12 . . causes 'C' to be written.

A program that will write a hexadecimal multiplication table uses this CASE statement. In addition it uses the identifiers DIV and MOD, which are part of Pascal's integer arithmetic. DIV divides integers and discards the remainder; a MOD 6 divides a by 6 and saves *only* the remainder (modular arithmetic).

```
PROGRAM hexatable (input,output);
VAR
    radix, column, rownum, entry: integer;
PROCEDURE hexwrite;
    VAR
        firstdigit, secdigit: integer;
    PROCEDURE hexchange (VAR digit: integer);
    BEGIN
        CASE digit of
            10:         write      ('A' : 1);
            11:         write      ('B' : 1);
            12:         write      ('C' : 1);
            13:         write      ('D' : 1);
            14:         write      ('E' : 1);
            15:         write      ('F' : 1);
            ELSE        write      (digit)
        END /* CASE digit */
    END /* hexchange */
```

```
BEGIN
    firstdigit: = entry DIV radix;
    hexchange (firstdigit);
    secdigit: = entry MOD radix;
    write ('        ')
END
BEGIN /* main program */
WRITE ('Enter radix for table = <16 ...        )';
READ (radix);
FOR rownum: = 1 TO radix −1 DO
    BEGIN
        entry: = rownum * column;
        hexwrite
    END; /* of entry calculation */
END. /* hexatable*
```

Figure 5-5 shows the results of running this program with radix = 16.

This brief section has only scratched the surface of Pascal's capabilities. We have not discussed the type sets, which permit the use of set algebra, or the type RECORD, which are structured variables like arrays but which may have components of different types, each accessed by name, such as

> name
> address
> telephone no.
> age

```
ENTER RADIX FOR TABLE =< 16... 16

01 02 03 04 05 06 07 08 09 0A 0B 0C 0D 0E 0F
02 04 06 08 0A 0C 0E 10 12 14 16 18 1A 1C 1E
03 06 09 0C 0F 12 15 18 1B 1E 21 24 27 2A 2D
04 08 0C 10 14 18 1C 20 24 28 2C 30 34 38 3C
05 0A 0F 14 19 1E 23 28 2D 32 37 3C 41 46 4B
06 0C 12 18 1E 24 2A 30 36 3C 42 48 4E 54 5A
07 0E 15 1C 23 2A 31 38 3F 46 4D 54 5B 62 69
08 10 18 20 28 30 38 40 48 50 58 60 68 70 78
09 12 1B 24 2D 36 3F 48 51 5A 63 6C 75 7E 87
0A 14 1E 28 32 3C 46 50 5A 64 6E 78 82 8C 96
0B 16 21 2C 37 42 4D 58 63 6E 79 84 8F 9A A5
0C 18 24 30 3C 48 54 60 6C 78 84 90 9C A8 B4
0D 1A 27 34 41 4E 5B 68 75 82 8F 9C A9 B6 C3
0E 1C 2A 38 46 54 62 70 7E 8C 9A A8 B6 C4 D2
0F 1E 2D 3C 4B 5A 69 78 87 96 A5 B4 C3 D2 E1
```

Figure 5–5   Output of program "hexatable."

and so on. RECORD gives Pascal much of the capability of COBOL. We have also not discussed files, which are extensions or (input, output). A good reference to Pascal containing these topics for further study is Grogono's book.[16]

REFERENCES

1   *Mini-Micro Systems* **13**, 105 (June 1980).

2   Krieger, M. S., and Planger, P. J., *Electronics*, **53**, 131–132 (May 8, 1980).

3   McGowan, M. J., *Control Engineering*, **27**, 53–58 (April 1980).

4   McCracken, D. D., *A Guide To Fortran Programming*, New York: Wiley (1965).

5   _____, *A Guide To PL/M Programming For Microcomputer Application*, Reading, Mass.: Addison-Wesley (1978).

6   Rather, E. D., and Moore, C. H., "FORTH High Level Programming Technique on Microprocessors," Electro 76, Boston, Mass. (May 11–14, 1976).

7   FORTH, Inc., Hermosa Beach, Calif.

8   Whitesmiths, Ltd., Systems Div., New York, N.Y. 10019.

9   Kernighan, B. W., and Ritchie, D. M., *The C Programming Language*, Englewood, Cliffs, N.J.: Prentice-Hall (1978).

10 Ritchie, D. M., Johnson, S. C.; Lesk, M. E., and Wernighan, B. W., *Bell System Technical Journal*, **57**, 1991–2019 (July–August,1978).

11 Jensen, K., and Werth, N., *Pascal User Manual And Report*, 2nd ed., New York: Springer-Verlag, (1979).

12 Posa, J., *Electronics*, 81–84 (October 12, 1978).

13 The Microengine Co., Newport Beach, Calif.

14 Dynasoft Systems, Windsor, Ontario, Canada.

15 _____, *ESI Pascal Language Instruction Manual*, Portland, Oregon: Electro Scientific Industries (1979).

16 Grogono, P., *Programming in Pascal*, Reading, Mass.: Addison-Wesley (1978).

6

Display

Outputting the results of computer operations is clearly of as much importance as the computer operations themselves. The visual presentation of these results represents one of many means of communicating computer output to the user. For large computer systems alphabetic and numeric data are probably the primary path for computer output. However, when tasks such as process control, telephone switching, automobile emission control, navigation, television color correction, and building climate control are considered, it is realized that computer output is used and made sensible in a large number of different ways. This chapter is concerned with but one of the means by which computer output is used: transient visual displays. Specifically, these are displays using lights, symbol generators, and cathode ray tube presentations. These output technologies are conventionally grouped together as display devices. Cathode ray tube devices are called CRTs or, more generally, *visual display units* (VDU).

Two classes of application considerations affect the design of the display subsystem. The first set deals with efficiently interfacing the display with the processor, the second set with interfacing the display with the human. The man-machine considerations dictate that the display must operate at speeds that are consistent with human capabilities and that it operate in human-compatible environments. Thus displays may be required to be usable in direct sunlight or perhaps at temperatures as cold as -20°F. However, operating extremes of temperature may for most civilian purposes be eliminated from consideration for this technology. Industrial or commercial computer displays are usually located in a room comfortable for operators. It should be noted in passing that much attention has been given to the psychological and anthropomorphic aspects of display design. These considerations have been found to enhance the ability of human operators to deal with large amounts of computer generated data with minimal error and fatigue. Optimizing these considerations is particularly important in many aerospace and military situations.

The human visual response time is both a problem and an aid to the display designer. The latency inherent in the human visual system allows a CRT (TV) display to be refreshed at a fairly slow rate while still providing the appearance of a continuous flickerfree picture. On the other hand human slowness relative to electronic speeds requires either that the processor slow down or that the display system provide temporary data storage which the processor can then rapidly and intermittently update. In almost all cases the system choice is the provision of temporary data storage capability associated with the display device.

ON-OFF DISPLAY

ON-OFF display, the simplest electronic visual output, was widely used with the earliest digital computing devices. The ON-OFF indication is commonly seen in two distinct types: as register bit display and as processor output port display. The most significant distinction between these two types of presentations lies in the degree of program (software) control that is exercised over the display. The register display commonly showing the last item on the address or data bus is generally a builtin function that is not under program control, while the output-port display is a computer function totally under program control. As an ON-OFF function the register display presents a binary number representing the individual bits on the bus. It gains in implementation simplicity what it loses in information convenience. The register displays on early computers were of great aid in initial debugging and subsequent maintenance of the hardware. Their primary application today is for tutorial purposes, many instruments, experimental controllers, and monitoring or troubleshooting functions.

Incandescent lamps, neon lamps, and light emitting diodes (LEDs) provide the illuminators for ON-OFF displays. The primary advantage associated with the incandescent lamp is the potential for maximum brightness. The disadvantages are relatively limited life and high illuminating current requirements. Typical current requirements for a low voltage lamp range from $1/10$ to several amperes; more illumination is of course obtained with more current. The large current requirements associated with the incandescent lamp necessitate a power driver. For currents in the range of $1/10$ ampere integrated circuit drivers may be used, while a transistor or a transistor Darlington circuit must be used for higher currents. The neon lamp provides the advantages of low current and long life. Its disadvantages are limited brightness and a need for a driver circuit having an open circuit voltage rating of at least 150 volts. At the present time the LED represents the most common choice for ON-OFF indicators. It has extremely long life, operates at currents of less than 20 milliamperes, is small in size, operates over a wide temperature range, and is available in red, green, and yellow. The LED has an operating voltage drop of around 0.6 volt. The under-20-milliampere current requirement, coupled with the low voltage drive requirement, permits the LED to be driven by an open collector TTL integrated circuit such as a 7401 type NAND gate. This circuit allows the further advantage of operation with the logic system voltage, thereby eliminating the need for an additional power supply.

Figure 6-1 shows an ON-OFF driver circuit employing a type 7401 TTL integrated circuit. The circuit combines an LED driver and a latch circuit function. The latch allows the indicator to retain its state after the processor has addressed and enabled the circuit, transferred the data

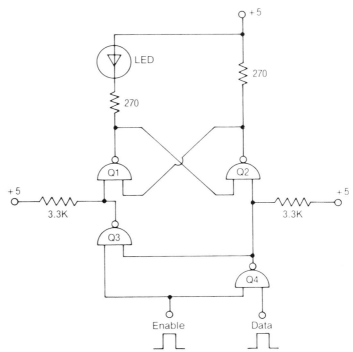

Figure 6–1   LED ON-OFF driver circuit.

state (HIGH or LOW signal) to the latch, and then disabled the circuit. This type of circuit takes advantage of the fact that a typical TTL type digital integrated logic package (DIP) contains four NAND gates within the single package. Thus, one DIP package and four resistors represent the total requirement to implement the driver circuit. In the circuit shown in Figure 6-1 NAND gates Q1 and Q2 with the characteristic flip-flop cross-coupled interconnections provide the latch function. NAND gates Q3 and Q4 provide the means for transferring the data state from the processor into the latch. The circuit is enabled by a positive signal that is generally derived from an address decoding circuit. When the circuit is enabled, a positive data signal causes the output of gate Q4 to be LOW, which results in gate Q1 to be ON and the LED to conduct current and produce light. Similarly, if the data signal were LOW, gate Q2 would switch to ON and the LED would be OFF. The cross-coupled connections between gates Q1 and Q2 allow the Q1-Q2 latch circuit to remain in its last enabled state after the enabling signal is removed. Of course, a flip-flop circuit module can be used in place of the developed latch.

CHARACTER DISPLAY

Character displays showing either numbers or words provide the next level of digital display sophistication. The presentation of information in the form of decimal numbers or simple words is clearly more understandable to humans than is a binary display. The two basic formats for character displays are dot matrix and multisegment. A subset of dots or segments is "illuminated" for the display of each character. Usually a number of character displays are grouped together to form a number or message. A particular system may contain several different groupings, all driven from a common computer bus.

CHARACTER TECHNOLOGY

The two dominant display technologies are LEDs and liquid crystal displays (LCDs). The LED displays generate their own light from the individual diode junctions that make up the display module. These LED displays, when used indoors (or in shaded environments), provide a very attractive, highly reliable display. The disadvantages associated with LED displays are that they fade out in very bright ambient conditions and have relatively high current requirements of 140 to 200 milliamperes per display word. The LCD provides a somewhat less dazzling display. It operates with either transmitted or reflected light, and consequently works well in normal and in very bright viewing environments. The LCD requires very little current to operate, typically a few tens of microamperes per display word. The most significant disadvantages of the LCD technology are that its response time decreases with falling temperature and that it does not easily accommodate multiplexing, thereby requiring more driver electronics than an equivalent LED display.

The seven-segment display represents the most common approach to the display of numbers. It is easily implemented with just three components and is readily controlled by the data bus. Figure 6-2 illustrates the 10 numbers that can be formed by a seven segment display. Figure 6-3 shows the circuit plan for control of the seven segments. The 10 possible decimal digits that can be displayed by the circuit are controlled by 4 bits of data received from the data bus. A 4-bit latch is used to store the 4-bit data word, permitting a long display time without monopolizing the computer system or the data bus. Data bits are loaded in parallel into the latch at a time determined by the address decoder and strobe signal. The 4 bits of data stored by the latch circuit are applied continuously to the input of the seven-segment decoder driver circuit module.

The seven-segment decoder driver typified by the SN7447 part is a circuit specifically designed for character display applications. The circuit is specialized in three ways to adapt it to the needs of character

Figure 6–2   Seven segment display numerals.

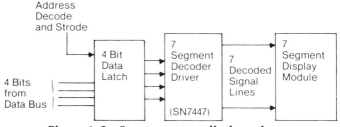

Figure 6–3   Seven-segment display scheme.

display: (1) It has open collector output circuits. (2) Each of these output circuits has the ability to sink 20 milliamperes of current, making it possible for each circuit to directly drive one LED of the display module at its maximum brightness. (3) Finally, the decoder is modified from the standard decoder function discussed in Chapter 1 to better fit the needs of the seven-segment display function. In the seven-segment decoder each output circuit corresponds to one of the display module segments. Each of the 16 combinations of the 4-bit input signal activates *several* of the segment driver output circuits to produce the desired segment pattern rather than a single one of the seven segments. Thus each input number code produces a unique output signal set rather than one signal.

The display module has one end of each segment connected in common. The other end is then available for direct connection to an output line from the seven-segment decoder. In an LED display it is obviously convenient for all the anode ends of the segments to be connected in common and to the positive supply voltage. Then the cathode end of each segment is connected to the open collector, output lines of the decoder. Thus every time a decoder output transistor is turned ON, and LED segment is illuminated. This situation is illustrated in Figure 6-4, where the ON connections for the display of the number 3 are shown in full lines and the OFF elements are shown dashed.

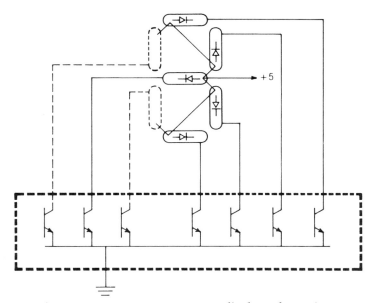

Figure 6–4   LED seven-segment display schematic.

LCDs interface to the data bus in a manner similar to LEDs, however, the phenomenon on which the display is based differs significantly. The LED creates light at its semiconductor diode junctions; the LCD alters external light which falls on it. LCD-type displays can operate in either a transmissive or reflective mode. The tranmissive mode is used when the display is backlighted, and the reflected mode relies on the ambient light surrounding the display. The reflective mode thus has excellent sunlight readability characteristics. The standard reflective display produces black digits on silver-gray reflective backgrounds, but other reflective background colors can be produced. The displays are readable at angles up to 60 degrees from the display normal.

LCDs employ an electrically controlled light polarizing phenomenon that is inherent in certain liquid crystal materials. Figure 6-5 illustrates the elements of an LCD. In this figure light generated at the left first passes through a vertical polarizer. The vertically polarized light then strikes the active portion of the display, the liquid crystal cell. The cell material has the ability to rotate the plane of polarization of light passing through it by 90 degrees. This rotated light is then able to pass through the second horizontal polarizer and then either passes through the transflector in the transmissive mode or is reflected by the rear reflector in the reflective mode. In the reflective mode the whole process is repeated a second time as the light reflects back through the polarizers and the liquid crystal cell to the viewer. The liquid crystal cell has transparent, electrically conductive segments deposited on its inside surfaces. When such a segment has an electric field imposed on it, the ability of the liquid crystal to rotate light is destroyed in the region of that segment. The transmitted light then cannot pass through the second polarizer, and the segment appears black because of an absence of light in the segment area.

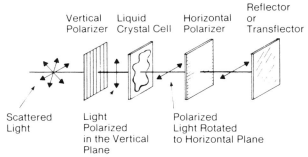

Figure 6–5   LCD elements.

In contrast to the LED, LCDs are driven by an AC voltage with a frequency between 25 and 100 hertz. The AC signal is used to maintain an electric field across the display. A DC voltage applied to the conductive surfaces would cause a decomposition of the liquid in the cell, greatly shortening the life of the display. In operation the display backplane and the display segments are driven with separate square wave signals. OFF segments are driven with square wave signals that are in phase with the backplane signal. ON segments are driven with square wave signals that are 180 degrees out of phase with the backplane drive. Thus for a backplane driven between ground and +10 volts, an ON segment would be driven to +10 volts when the backplane is zero and would be at zero when the backplane is at +10 volts. These conditions are illustrated in Figure 6-6. It can be seen that an OFF segment has no field across it, while an ON segment has an applied field that is constantly changing directions. Thus there is no average DC field across a segment at any time.

An electro-optical delay is characteristic of LCDs. When an AC voltage is applied to the display, a field is generated which exerts a force on the liquid crystal molecules that causes the molecules to physically move. The movement is not instantaneous; rather they move at a rate dependent on the temperature of the liquid and the strength of the applied field. The colder the liquid the longer the time required for the molecules to reorient to different field conditions. The lower operating temperature limit for an LCD is set by the temperature at which the LCD response time becomes unacceptably long.

MULTIPLEXING

In the context of digital displays, multiplexing refers to the technique of using a single set of decoder driver logic to operate several or all of the digits of a display. The LED display, because of the high speed of

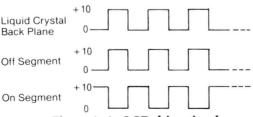

Figure 6-6   LCD drive signals.

response of the light emitting diode, adapts to multiplexing very nicely. A single set of decoder drivers drives all the display segments in parallel. However, separate digital drivers select only one digit of the display at a time. Thus the decoder drivers can only effectively activate the segments of the selected digit, and only a single decoder driver circuit is needed for the full display. This multiplexing process relies on the latent image effect of the eye to produce an apparently steady display. With a common anode display element, as illustrated in Figure 6-4, the digit select, multiplexing switch would be connected to the common anode while the single decoder driver would connect in parallel to the appropriate segments of all the characters of the display.

Because the transition time for an LCD display is on the order of 100 milliseconds, it adapts much less readily to multiplexing. Several LCD characteristics make the device difficult to multiplex. Three interrelated parameters must be considered.*

1. Reduced operating temperature range.
2. Reduced viewing cone.
3. Reduced flexibility.

The amount of multiplexing that still results in an acceptable display is more a function of the user's environment than of any display parameter that can be controlled. Multiplex ratios of eight characters to one driver are found to be satisfactory for toys. Other uses such as automotive applications restrict acceptable multiplexing drives to two or three characters per driver.

CRT DISPLAY

The CRT provides the basis for the most flexible of all the computer output display devices. This tube can be used to display arbitrary combinations of numbers, text, line drawings, and more elaborate graphics. The CRT is best known as the "picture tube" in the home television set. The enormous production capacity that has been built up to support the television industry has produced as an offshoot the inexpensive computer display. Indeed, the common home television set is used to provide a very satisfactory computer display, thus providing a remarkable function at a very low cost. For display of more than 40 characters per line,

*Riordan, Keith, "LCD Multiplexing Perplexing?" *Fairchild Journal of Semiconductors*, **8** (1), (January/February 1980).

the resolution of home video receivers is unsatisfactory, and special CRT monitors are required.

CRTs can display up to several thousand characters at the same time. They can therefore be seen as the ultimate in multiplexed character displays. Character multiplexing on the CRT face takes advantage of the slow response, latency effect of the eye. However, the CRT display also uses to advantage the relatively persistent decay characteristics of its phosphor to effectively provide a large short-term picture memory.

Figure 6-7 provides a schematic representation of a CRT. The tube is a glass enclosed vacuum bottle that generates electrons at its smaller end (left) and displays visual information on the light generating phosphor located on the inside surface of its face, shown at the right of the figure. The tube operates in a high vacuum so that the electrons can travel, unimpeded by gas molecules, from the cathode to the faceplate of the tube. When an electron strikes the phosphor layer on the face of the tube, the phosphor molecules are electronically excited to a higher energy state. When these molecules spontaneously return to their normal energy levels, they emit photons of light which are visible to the eye. Each type of phosphor has its own set of energy states, resulting in unique colors and differing rates of decay. By careful selection and mixing of phosphors, many desirable characteristics of color and persistence can be obtained.

Electrons are generated at the cathode element of the tube. The

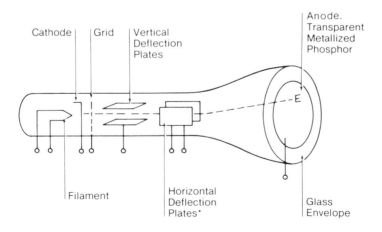

* Or External Magnetic Coils

Figure 6–7   Schematic of cathode ray tube (CRT).

filament heats the cathode and produces a rich supply of electrons. The anode electrode of the CRT is associated with the phosphor and is operated at a high positive voltage with respect to the cathode. Typical operating anode voltages are 5000 to 20,000 volts. The high potential difference between the cathode and the anode of the tube accelerates free electrons from the cathode to the anode. For the tube to provide a useful display it is important that this electron beam be collimated and focused to provide a fine spot at the phosphor surface. Grid electrodes located near the cathode produce electric fields that form the beam. The entire assembly is called an *electron gun.* Depending on the design of the tube, visual spot diameters in the range of 0.001 to 0.02 inches can be obtained. The spot size determines the resolution of the tube and limits the number and quality of graphic characters that can be written on the tube face.

Grid electrodes provide another very important function in the CRT, that of modulating the density of the cathode to anode electron beam. The control grid thus determines the brightness of the display. It also can be driven dynamically to totally cut off the electron beam to the phosphor. This intensity or *Z axis modulation* is used to blank the television tube during periods when it is desired to move the beam but to avoid drawing extraneous lines between characters and portions of characters.

The focused beam of electrons is simultaneously deflected vertically and horizontally by the respective deflection plates shown in Figure 6-7 or by alternative magnetic coils (see below). A differential voltage is applied across a pair of plates to move the beam. A voltage on a deflection plate that is more positive than the beam potential will attract the beam toward it, while a relatively negative potential will repel the beam. The deflection sensitivity in terms of centimeters of deflection per applied deflection volt depends on the separation of the plates and the "stiffness" of the beam, which is dependent on the potential difference between anode and cathode. The greater this potential difference, the stiffer the beam is and the harder it is to deflect.

The deflection mechanism described with the aid of Figure 6-7 has been described in terms of electric fields produced by voltage applied to physical deflection plates. But it should be noted that the electron beam can also be focused and deflected by magnetic fields generated by electrically driven coils located external to the tube interior. This approach simplifies the construction of the CRT at a cost of adding the external deflection and/or focusing coils. Indeed, this approach is the one selected for high volume manufacture in the television industry. However, the concepts of display generation, Z axis modulation, and focusing are basically the same for computer display devices.

CHARACTER GENERATION

Two basic techniques are used to generate characters on a CRT: vector and raster generation. Either technique can produce poor to excellent figures depending on the resolution of the spot size and the elements used to form them.

Vector techniques depend on the ability of the CRT display system to locate the beam at any selected position on the CRT face. From the starting position a series of short connected line segments or vectors are generated which cause the beam to trace out a path representing the desired figure. This technique is illustrated in Figure 6-8. The beam is Z axis modulated to its OFF condition when portions of the traversed path are not to be drawn on the screen, and brightened when the figure is traced. This technique is attractive when there are relatively few characters to be displayed and very high speed is required. It may also be attractive when the vector line segment generator is required for drawing a variety of figures that have either nonstandard shapes or a variety of sizes. A major disadvantage associated with the vector technique is the broadband requirements placed on the vertical and horizontal deflection amplifiers. These amplifiers must often be designed to have a low frequency response down to DC in addition to having excellent zero

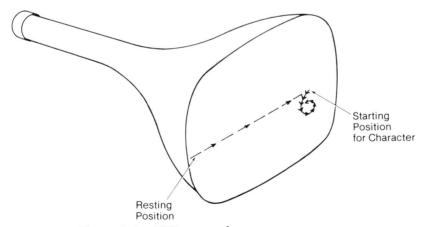

Figure 6–8   **CRT vector character generator.**

and gain stability and as high a frequency response as can be practically obtained (usually in the range of 500 kilohertz to 2 megahertz).

The most common type of CRT display system employs a television type of raster scan. With this technique the CRT beam is continuously deflected over the entire face of the CRT, as shown in Figure 6-9.

In an actual TV scan the tilt of the raster is very small, and hundreds of horizontal raster scans occupy a single pass over the face of the CRT. In this scheme the time interval required for each horizontal scan is a constant, thereby allowing any location on the raster to be determined by the time interval measured from the start of the scan. Thus with a fixed raster scanning the tube (i.e., deflecting the CRT electron beam) the information to be displayed is contained within a single stream of video data that can be used to modulate the brightness of the display. For a computer display, where no gray scale is required, the beam modulation is strictly a binary, ON-OFF operation. A video signal for such a display is thus very readily generated by conventional binary logic circuits. The bandwidth of the video channel is another limiting factor in graphic resolution and, depending on the number of characters per line, lies in the range of 7 to 20 megahertz. However, since the circuits deal only with binary signals, the required design is much easier to implement than the wideband analog amplifiers demanded by the vector system.

The economics of large scale production make the conventional television chassis very attractive for computer display. For the personal computer system, a television system is usually available and the inter-

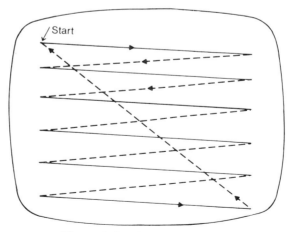

Figure 6–9   CRT raster scan

face requirement is nothing more complicated than the connection of a signal modulator between the computer and the antenna terminals of the TV set. These RF modulators are available at low cost from retail electronic and personal computer stores.

For the computer manufacturer the TV chassis is also attractive. With the radio section removed, the TV chassis can be purchased in quantity at a very low price, and the manufactured system can be designed to use the video signal directly, without a modulator.

A TV requirement that is retained in both the personal and professional TV raster displays is the incorporation of vertical and horizontal synchronization signals in the video signal stream; this is known as *composite video.* With respect to Figure 6-9 the synchronizing signal initiates the horizontal deflection at the point labeled START. At the same time the vertical deflection is also started. The horizontal deflection signal moves the beam across the face of the CRT to the right edge of the picture. At this point a *flyback signal* returns the beam to the left edge. During the flyback time the tube is blanked by Z modulation so that no line is drawn. Each successive horizontal scan cycle is initiated by a horizontal synchronization signal. The vertical deflection signal initiated at the start of the raster cycle continues while the horizontal scan cycle covers a progressively lower place on the CRT face. A TV format actually requires two raster cycles to fully scan the picture tube; that is, the TV format interlaces two sets of raster scans. This interlacing doubles the vertical resolution of the picture and at the same time minimizes the time lag between top of picture and bottom of picture scanning. Some TV format terminals generate the same video data for the interlaced scan as was used for the initial scan, while others distinguish between the two scans and effectively double the resolution of the display picture.

Figure 6-10 illustrates the manner in which a TV raster is used to generate character data. The CRT beam is intensified at selected times along each horizontal scan, producing the character image on the CRT

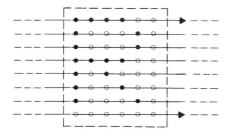

Figure 6–10   Raster-dot character generator using CRT.

face. This intensification (Z modulation) signal is the video signal. With each horizontal scan initiated by a synchronizing signal, the appropriate video signal is defined by a sequence of pulses having a specified time delay from the synchronization signal.

It is convenient to think of each character as being enclosed within a rectangular matrix box. These boxes then are packed tightly together on the face of the CRT to form the available display character space. In the example shown in Figure 6-10 the basic character is shown defined by a matrix of dots that is seven rows high and five rows wide. An extra row and column are included within the conceptual character box to provide separation between adjacent characters when they are packed into a standard display. Thus the display box is actually a 6 × 8 matrix. The character within each display box is defined by a code convention, usually the ASCII code (see Table 3-2), and the CRT display space is mapped into a corresponding memory space. That is, each display box has an associated display memory location, and scanning along rows of displayed characters is equivalent to sequentially reading out the display memory (using sequential memory addresses). The painting of a row of character data proceeds scan by scan. Thus each code for each character on the line (including SPACE) is read from memory eight times as the eight rows of dots, corresponding to the single row of displayed characters, are painted.

Because the characters painted onto the CRT face by the electron beam remain visible for only a few tens of milliseconds (as is the case with most multiplexed displays), the presentation of a stable, flickerfree picture requires a continuous refresh of the display. If the picture must be continuously repainted, the display memory must be continuously accessed. It is common in the United States to use a display refresh rate of 60 times per second. The use of a refresh rate equal to that of the AC power frequency minimizes the effect on the CRT display of power line hum pickup. A 1000-character display space painted at a rate of 60 times per second allots approximately 12 microseconds for each character (allowing for flyback time). Reading out the refresh memory once per display box row per character, or eight times per character, indicates that the memory must be accessed every 1.5 microseconds for character data. This utilization rate for the display memory dictates that the CRT display system incorporate its own refresh memory and that this memory have a capacity at least equal to the CRT display space.

The processor driving the CRT system, which may be itself a microprocessor, deals with character codes that are transferred from the processor memory system to the refresh memory of the CRT system. The display system must transform each character code into an appropriate video signal. This basic transformation is made with a ROM chip that employs the character codes as addresses and whose data output is ones and zeros corresponding to the desired video pattern. A typical ROM character generator such as the 2513 is organized so that a 9-bit address is applied to the chip. It uses 6 of these bits to address 64 different character patterns and 3 bits to address any one of the eight rows making up the matrix pattern of the addressed character. The 3-bit row address, generated by the control and timing circuitry, causes the synchronizing signals to be generated and generally controls the overall function of the CRT display.

CRT TERMINALS

CRT terminals all provide the basic function of entering and displaying alphanumeric data. The video display function alone, without keyboard or character generation, is termed a *monitor.* CRT terminals differ from printers in their ability to rapidly modify the displayed data and in their avoidance of generating a mountain of paper. By definition the basic display technology is the CRT; however, other technologies such as the plasma panel and large LCD panels are beginning to provide competitive technologies. For the present at least the CRT serves the overwhelming majority of terminal display applications, and we focus on this mode of display in the remainder of this chapter.

A wide spectrum of CRT terminals are available, ranging from the simplest form of a television receiver to sophisticated multifunction systems. The personal computer user constrained by cost provides an example of the most basic terminal, where the monitor itself is simply a commercial television receiver. The Ohio Scientific CI-P personal computer provides an excellent example of this type of system. Here the video refresh logic, the character generator, and the associated timing control logic are all located on the same assembly as the processor, and the connection to the terminal is simply a single coaxial wire. Another such integrated system is the Synertek KTM-2, which operates in conjunction with the SYM-1 single board microcomputer. The KTM-2 is produced in two versions: at 40 characters per line, using a TV receiver, or 80 characters per line, requiring a higher resolution video monitor.

With the CI-P, data that are being displayed by the TV receiver are stored in the video RAM and continuously cycled out from the memory to the character generator under control of the video timing and control logic.

The data are sequentially read out of the video memory merely by providing a continuous stream of sequential addresses to the memory. The codes read from the memory are applied to the character generator, which in turn generates the binary video pattern appropriate to the code. The video memory receives address data from two sources: from the video timing logic during normal display processing, and from the processor address bus when the video memory is being loaded from the processor data bus. The video data generated by the character generator are mixed with the periodic television vertical and horizontal synchronizing signals. This composite video signal then leaves the processor board. In the simplest TV set interconnection scheme the composite video signal is passed through a simple modulator circuit assembly, and the modulator output signal is then connected directly to the antenna terminals of the TV receiver. The modulator imposes the video signals on a TV RF carrier signal. The receiver is then tuned to the station setting corresponding to the carrier frequency of the modulator, and the system is complete.

The modulator can be a simple off-the-shelf one-transistor circuit assembly. If a modulator is not used, the composite video signal must be introduced into the TV circuitry at a point following the RF tuning section and before the sync signals are detected. In this approach care must be taken to ensure that high voltage TV set potentials are fully isolated from the processor circuits.

The circuitry required to effect the basic CRT terminal function is essentially the same whether the circuitry is located with the CRT or with the processor. However, when only a single terminal is involved, as in the single-board, personal computer example, substantial gains can be made by locating the circuitry with the processor. Specifically, by making use of the processor address bus, the control required for loading the video RAM from the processor is greatly simplified. The interconnections of the address and data buses with the video RAM are greatly simplified when all the circuits are located on the same printed circuit card and when the video circuitry is able to share the processor power supply.

The disadvantages associated with combining the processor and video circuitry are seen when it is desired to have more than one CRT terminal in the system. Often the video circuitry associated with even one system becomes so large because of added video features that it does not conveniently fit on the space available on the simple processor printed circuit board.

Terminals that have their associated video refresh memories located remotely from the host processor usually communicate with the processor through a two-wire, serial communication protocol (e.g., RS-232).

The simplification of interconnection wiring associated with serial transmission carries with it the burden of the parallel to serial conversion process at each end of the channel and reduced processor speed when the processor is involved in the serial transmission process.

SMART TERMINALS

The CRT terminal is commonly an operator-attended data input station as well as output station. To aid the operator with the data input task, additional features are often added to the terminal; these features create what has come to be known as the *smart terminal*. The types of features associated with the smart terminal are foreground/background displays, split screen displays, reverse video, blinking, upper- and lowercase letters, and special input plotting and input formating controls. Color is also a significant attribute of many displays.

Foreground/background displays are particularly useful when the terminal operator enters data onto a form. With this feature the background display can be the form itself, while the input data can be the foreground data. In this type of dual field display the background data can be write-protected against inadvertent alteration (writing over the data), while the foregound data can be input or changed by keyboard actions.

Split screen displays divide the display area into two or more independent message displays. This type of format is useful in word-processing applications such as language translation and editing, or where it is desired to display operating instructions next to some kind of data display. The split screen display is another type of protected area display, and uses the same implementation required for foreground/background displays.

Reverse video, a feature often found in black and white displays, provides the capability of reversing the background and foreground color for a specified segment of text display. Thus a display having light characters on a dark (nonilluminated) background with reverse video would show dark characters (nonilluminated) on a bright (illuminated background). This feature is used to highlight selected portions of the display. It is an attractive feature from an implementation point because it provides a useful capability with very little circuitry. It is only necessary to invert the generated video stream before it is combined with the synchronizing signals. Adding to the logic to add or remove the requisite inverter under program control is all that is required to provide this capability.

Blinking is another display feature that is used to highlight a portion of the display message. It is implemented by periodically supressing the video corresponding to the characters under blink control, at a slow multiple of the video frame rate. The implementation of this feature is also very straightforward. The most significant bit of a 7- or 8-bit counter that is repetitively counting vertical synchronization signals is combined with the blink control signal to provide a half-on, half-off signal at an appropriately slow rate.

The use of both upper- and lowercase letters requires having both upper- and lowercase video patterns built into the character generator ROM. With this type of implementation both patterns are drawn within the same dot matrix pattern box. When using minimal character matrix sizes such as 6 × 8, some compromise with style is accepted. Upper- and lowercase letters are represented within the standard ASCII code set, so the utilization of at least a 6-bit ASCII subcode set provides 64 different patterns, adequate capability for specifying the upper- and lowercase characters.

Plotting represents one of the major attributes of CRT-based systems. The voltage driven CRT (analog) display space appears to offer the potential for unlimited resolution. But in practice even the most sophisticated displays have a resolution along a major axis of 1 part in 1000. Most high quality CRT terminals provide a line of 80 characters and from 25 to 48 lines per frame. On the basis of the 6 × 8 character matrix (Figure 6-10) the basic resolution of the terminal can be characterized as 480 points horizontally and 200 to 386 points vertically, providing 96,000 to 185,000 *pixels* (picture/elements). However, the available plotting resolution in most terminals is not usually this fine. "Limited graphics" terminals approach plotting by dividing each character box into a number of subunits which is less than the resolution provided by the points of the character matrix.

The ISC (Intelligent Systems Corp.) 8001 terminal, for example, divides each character box into an 8-pixel, 2 × 4 plotting space, providing a horizontal resolution of 160 (2 × 80) and a vertical resolution of 100 (2 × 35 for 35 line systems). Thus a modestly priced system that is specifically oriented toward graphic information display is obtained, providing a basic plotting resolution of 160 × 100 (expandable to 160 × 140) pixels.

Using somewhat the same concept, the low cost OSI CI-P personal computer allows the character box to be divided into a 2 × 2, 4-pixel space, but the CI-P provides only a 25-character, 25-line display format, so the available basic resolution is 50 × 50 pixels. In alternate modes this system can use a 1 × 8 or an 8 × 1 division of each character space, producing a resolution of 200 × 25 (or 25 × 200) pixels. However, only a single horizontal line can be drawn through the character box at this resolution. The ISC system, by contrast, provides that any combination of the 8 pixels within a character box may be selected simultaneously.

The approach to plotting taken by the CI-P system is interesting in that enhanced plotting resolution is obtained without any added hardware complexity through the stratagem of providing special graphics characters that are built into the ROM of the character generator. Thus by adding the set of 6 patterns seen in Figure 6-11, the plotting resolution for simple drawings is increased by a factor of 4 over that provided by the character box. The strategy is seriously limited, however, by practical considerations; that is, all possible patterns are not usable. In a character set for 3 × 3 division of the character box there are 84 combinations of 9 elements taken 3 at a time. Of these possibilities, approximately 23 patterns can be eliminated by being internally contiguous, leaving about 61 possibilities.

Further extensions of the technique of using special character ROM for enhancing plotting resolution would have to go to a more complicated strategy such as establishing a plotting mode where double characters are used to call up simple video combinations from the character ROM on a row by row basis.

Different types of plotting applications require varying degrees of

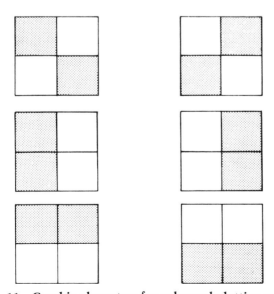

Figure 6–11 Graphic characters for enhanced plotting resolution.

plotting resolution. Histograms represent one of the simplest plotting applications and require minimal resolution. The plotting of a distribution of data within a measurement space is likely to present the next level of resolution requirement, followed by applications involving the plotting of analytic functions. The most severe resolution requirements seem to be associated with aesthetics of artistic material and the physical requirements of mechanical drawings in computer-aided design (CAD). A printed circuit board, for example, is often plotted at a magnification of 4 using a grid spacing of 0.1 or 0.05 inches. Thus an 8 × 10 inch board would require a plotting space of either 320 × 400 or 640 × 800 pixels. The resolution requirements for plotting integrated circuit design layouts are significantly greater. The approach taken by sophisticated CAD systems is to provide good resolution on the basic CRT and extreme resolution through the technique of "zooming in" on small areas. Here a large amount of memory is required to store the entire set of pixels, but the display can present the total scene at modest resolution, thereby allowing the operator to view any portion of the drawing in appropriate detail.

Color provides a major aesthetic enhancement for CRT displays. Often the colored display is provided by a basic color television receiver. The provision of color information along with the video data represents a complication of the terminal interface. However, if a television signal format is used, the video data can be transmitted to the display as a single serial data stream connected to the CRT system through a single coaxial cable. The standard TV receiver already contains circuitry for separating the incoming data stream into parallel video, color, and synchronization data channels.

Three basic analog signal channels provide all the information required by the color television receiver. These signals are luminance, color A, and color B. They are provided to the receiver as two-carrier (modulated RF) signals. The luminance signal combines the basic picture, vertical, and horizontal synchronization information. The luminance signal is similar to the signal received by a standard black and white television receiver, and is tuned to the desired receiver channel. Color information is transmitted as a 2.579545-megahertz subcarrier chroma signal in parallel with the luminance signal. It is transmitted as a phase shift signal imposed on the chroma subcarrier. The addition of the luminance and modulated chroma signal results in the RF signal that can be accepted by the color television receiver.

A direct means of providing a color television signal interface is through the use of color TV video modulator integrated circuit MC1372, manufactured by Motorola Semiconductor. A block diagram of the circuit is seen in Figure 6-12*A*. Figure 6-12*B* shows the circuit along with the external components required to provide a complete color modulator circuit. The MC1372 provides still another example of the ability of the integrated circuit to provide sophisticated functions in small packages of modest cost.

The utilization of color or high resolution plotting capabilities with a CRT terminal necessarily requires the transmission of more data between the processor and the display than is required by a simple terminal. The problem for the CRT terminal design is compounded by the dual objectives of providing a protocol that is efficient for the host processor and also efficient for the human operator who may be providing data to the terminal through a keyboard.

The ISC 8001 terminal approaches this problem by providing multiple modes of operation. It is possible for the terminal to operate in two different modes simultaneously: one mode that controls data input from the host computer that enters through the serial RS-232 port, and a second mode that affects data entered from the keyboard. The refresh memory associated with the CRT display is organized as two 8-bit bytes per display character. One byte carries the ASCII code, and the second byte carries the information for blink control and background and foreground color. This format provides full color control on a character by character basis.

When the terminal is in the *protect mode,* discrimination between protected and unprotected information is made on the basis of the data color. This technique not only is useful for entering data but also is used for selective transmission out of the terminal of unprotected data. Within the protect mode umbrella a number of standard functions such as cursor home, line feed, tab, erase, and carriage return operate, but only on the unprotected data. Thus a tab function would operate to move the point of next data entry (the cursor) from its present position in an unprotected data area to the start of the next unprotected data field. When data are transmitted from the protect mode, the second data byte containing the blink and color information is stripped away and only the ASCII data codes are sent out.

Plotting on the 8001 terminal is done with the aid of the *plot mode.* A number of special submodes all have the effect of placing colored squares within the character box. Special plot modes also permit alphanumeric characters to be located along a vertical and 45-degree axis. The character plot discussed above provides the mechanism for dividing each character space into a 2×4 plotting matrix. The terminal provides the means for locating the plotting matrix either by specifying its *X-Y* character position or by incremental advancement of this plotting ma-

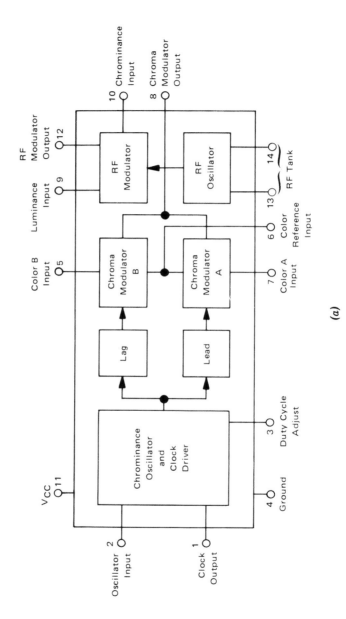

(a)

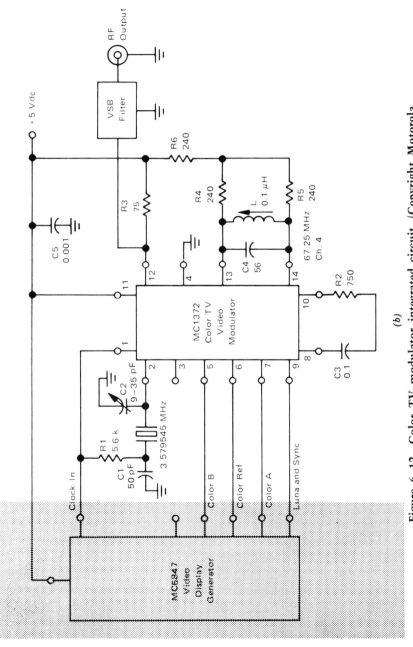

Figure 6–12 Color TV modulator integrated circuit. (Copyright Motorola Semiconductor Products Inc., (reproduced by permission.)

(b)

153

trix position from its last position. Still another mode permits the plot-ting matrix to be bypassed through the direct specification of any plot point within the expanded 160×100 (192) display space. This expanded space may also be accessed by another incremental plotting mode that accepts a sequential series of change in X, change in Y values. A final vector mode receives XY coordinate values for a starting point and a terminating point, and thereafter plots the best straight line between these points using the plot mode blocks.

Recent integrated circuit developments have seen the production of CRT controllers. These single chip devices, in association with their refresh memories, provide essentially all the circuitry required for a CRT terminal. Figure 6-13A shows a Motorola MC6847 integrated circuit CRT controller with Figure 6-13B defining the input pins of the IC. The entire video display control function is provided by this single 40-pin IC, which provides a display space of 256×192 pixels.

The alphanumeric display modes of the controller use a basic 8×12 dot character matrix and show a display of 16 lines with 32 characters per line. One of two colors for the light dots may be selected by the chip color set selector pin.

An internal character generator ROM can produce 64 ASCII charac-ters in a standard 5×7 matrix. Here 6 bits of the 8-bit data word are used for character selection and the remaining 2 bits can be used to imple-ment inverse video and color switching on a character by character basis. Included within the alphanumeric mode are two semigraphic modes, which provide enhanced resolution, as discussed earlier, for graphic plotting. Alpha Semigraphic 4 mode divides the 8×12 display box into 4 elements (each measuring 4×6 dots), providing a graphic

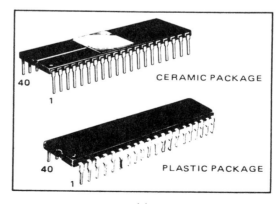

CERAMIC PACKAGE

PLASTIC PACKAGE

(*a*)

PIN ASSIGNMENT

Mnemonic	Pin Numbers	Function
V$_{CC}$	17	+5V
V$_{SS}$	1	Ground
CLK	33	Color burst clock 3.579545 MHz (input)
DA0-DA12	22, 23, 24, 25, 26, 13, 14, 15, 16, 18, 19, 20, 21	Address lines to display memory, high impedance during memory select ($\overline{MS}$)
DD0-DD5	3, 4, 5, 6, 7, 8	Data from display memory RAM or ROM
DD6, DD7	2, 40	Data from display memory in graphic mode; data also in alpha external mode; color data in alpha semigraphic 4 or 6
φA, φB, Y	11, 10, 28	Chrominance and luminance analog (R-Y, B-Y, Y) output to RF modulator (MC1372)
CHB	9	Chroma bias; reference φA and φB levels
$\overline{RP}$	36	Row preset – Output to provide timing for external character generator.
$\overline{HS}$	38	Horizontal Sync – Output to provide timing for external character generator.
INV	32	Inverts video in all alpha modes
$\overline{INT}$/EXT	31	Switches to external ROM in alpha mode and between SEMIG-4 and SEMIG-6 in semigraphics
$\overline{A}$/S	34	Alpha/Semigraphics; selects between alpha and semigraphics in alpha mode
$\overline{MS}$	12	Memory select forces VDG address buffers to high-impedance state
$\overline{A}$/G	35	Switches between alpha and graphic modes
$\overline{FS}$	37	Field Synchronization goes low at bottom of active display area.
CSS	39	Color set select; selects between two alpha display colors or between two color sets in semigraphics 6 and full graphics
GM0-GM2	30, 29, 27	Graphic mode select; select one of eight graphic modes.

ADI 492 R2

Figure 6–13 Integrated circuit CRT controller. (Copyright Motorola Semiconductor Products Inc., reproduced by permission.)

display with a resolution of 64 × 32 elements. Alpha Semigraphic 6 mode divides the 8 × 12 display box into 6 elements (each measuring 4 × 4 dots), providing a resolution of 64 × 48 elements.

The controller chip also provides five-color graphic modes ranging from a 64 × 64 pixel four-color mode to a 256 × 192 pixel two-color mode. Figure 6-14 provides a table summarizing the available modes of the MC6847 video display generator.

SUMMARY OF MAJOR MODES

Title	Memory	Colors	Display Elements
Alphanumeric (Internal)	512 x 8	2	
Alphanumeric (External)	512 x 8	2	
Alpha Semig-4	512 x 8	8	Box 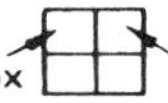 Element
Alpha Semig-6	512 x 8	4	Box 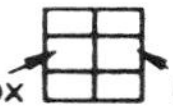 Element

Title	Memory	Colors	Comments
64 x 64 Color Graphic	1K x 8	. 4	Matrix 64 x 64 Elements
128 x 64 Graphics*	1K x 8	2	Matrix 128 elements wide by
128 x 64 Color Graphic	2K x 8	4	64 elements high
128 x 96 Graphics*	1.5K x 8	2	Matrix 128 elements wide by
128 x 96 Color Graphic	3K x 8	4	96 elements high
128 x 192 Graphics*	3K x 8	2	Matrix 128 elements wide by
128 x 192 Color Graphic	6K x 8	4	192 elements high
256 x 192 Graphics*	6K x 8	2	Matrix 256 elements wide by 192 elements high

*Graphics mode turns on or off each element. The color may be one of two.

Figure 6–14   Available modes of video display generator. (Copyright Motorola Semiconductor Products Inc., reproduced by permission.)

Within the set of microprocessor system functions the video display generator (VDG) is a noteworthy exception. Whereas all other system functions are under the direct control of a CPU and are activated through the selection of unique addresses in the address space of the system, the VDG is a free-running function that, like the processor, calls respectively on memory for data. Of course, the VDG only addresses that portion of memory reserved for the display memory, while the processor addresses the entire memory space of the system, but in terms of interaction with the memory space the VDG functions more like a processor than does the other peripheral output functions that comprise a microprocessor system and, as noted earlier, may actively incorporate a processor.

The CPU is the source of the data that resides in the display refresh memory, and it must consequently control the address space of the refresh memory when it is loading data into the memory (and when it is examining data already in the refresh memory). While the CPU is in control of this memory, the VDG addressing of the memory must be disabled. This is accomplished in the MC6847 by driving pin 12 to its LOW state. This condition forces the VDG address buffers to their high impedance state and effectively eliminates all VDG control of the refresh memory address lines. Disabling the VDG may cause unacceptable disturbances in the CRT display, but these can be avoided in a raster scan display by limiting processor access to the refresh memory to those times during which the CRT is normally blanked, that is, during the beam retrace times. For a standard television format this is the time allotted for the beam to retrace from the finish of a frame to the top of the next frame.

It is interesting to consider the functions provided by the single chip MC6847 compared with the substantial circuitry of the 8001 terminal. In general there is a general commonality of function provided by the two systems. The 8001 terminal provides more displayed characters and more color control. It provides less graphic resolution than is available from the MC6847. Perhaps the most significant difference lies in the fact that the VDG chip provides no mechanism for loading the refresh memory. Consequently, its repertoire of functions includes no cursor controls. For the VDG system these functions have to be associated with the computer or keyboard system that will provide the data its refresh memory.

7

Multiple Microprocessor Communication

There is much more to be said about the application of single microprocessors than we have covered in this book. However, it is important to recognize the accelerating growth of systems utilizing several or many microprocessors linked together in some fashion to achieve cooperative tasks. Their low cost encourages this multiple usage. A common case is the *smart terminal*, (see Chapter 6) which acts as an interface between a computer and a keyboard, video monitor, and perhaps other peripherals. A keyboard (Synertek KTM-2/80) used by one of the authors in conjunction with a 6502 single-board microprocessor in the preparation of this book has, in its own circuitry, two 6500 microprocessors; these control the formation of characters and graphics by intensity-modulating the monitor's video scan lines, control a cursor and RS-232C serial communications to a printer, and perform many other functions.[1]

More powerful systems include combinations of multiple microprocessors programmed to act as process controllers or as control/display stations for the operators of chemical plants, petroleum refineries, and power generating stations. Some examples of this type of application are given in Ref. (2). Very often these systems are expanded by incorporating layers of larger processors, such as 16- or 32-bit minicomputers, in hierarchal relationship to the microprocessors. The smaller machines then perform dedicated real-time functions, such as the calculation of process control algorithms or the generation and updating of displays and logs, while the larger processor performs functions requiring more computing power (speed and memory), such as optimization of the processes by linear programming. Figure 7-1 shows this relationship graphically.

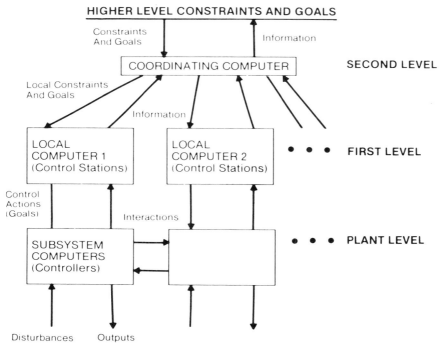

Figure 7–1   Distributed processors performing control functions in a plant. (Adapted from Kahne, Lefkowitz and Rose.[4])

DISTRIBUTED PROCESSORS

Generally speaking, there are three kinds of systems employing multiple processors. The first type, which is an extension of the smart terminal, is commonly used in electronic data processing (EDP) systems, and is termed *distributed processing* by EDP practitioners. In these applications many individual terminals in separate locations independently process transactions or perform computation tasks in conjunction with local processors (mini- or microcomputers) and local data bases (storage). They are linked to one or more central locations equipped with larger computers and central data bases that have the functions of summarizing and totalizing the outputs of their hierarchal satellites. The distributed functions of these systems, both geographical and taskwise, include data processing, the storage of information in data bases, and the communication of data. Many such EDP systems are found in multiple-branch banks and in larger retail stores. Examples of their use are found in standard EDP textbooks.[3]

The second type of distributed processing system is solely concerned with the computation and data processing functions of mainframe computers. These systems are not geographically distributed, but combine in one location the central processing function of several computers to form a single entity. The combined system is both more powerful and more reliable than its individual parts. The greater power comes from the ability to share tasks and to perform operations in parallel (hence more rapidly), while the greater reliability stems from the ability to dynamically reassign functions and to automatically switch from a failed processor to those remaining in operation without interrupting any of the tasks. Multiple processors of this type are called *closely coupled* because their functions are intimately tied together at a basic level of operation, that of the CPU. Consequently, the communication between individual parts must be at very high speed so as not to slow the nanosecond elementary operations of the arithmetic units within the individual processors. One example of this kind of coupling is found in the Honeywell Level 6 minicomputers, which utilize special "scientific" and "commercial" processors on the same parallel bus lines as the normal processor. If the main CPU recognizes a FORTRAN instruction, for example, it does not process it, but sends it to the scientific processor, which is optimized for this function. Likewise, a COBOL instruction would be sent to the commercial processor. These processors would then perform their task while the main CPUs go about other tasks in parallel.

It is obvious that in this kind of application the communication must be very rapid. In the application just described a parallel bus is used, but in some experimental close-coupled processors very high speed serial buses (10 megabits per second or better) are used. Often these are fiber optics links. We discuss the nature of such serial buses, but will not be concerned further with this kind of multiple processing. Although these systems may well utilize microprocessors, perhaps in large numbers, the theory of such large machines is presently in an early stage, and their operating and programming problems are quite beyond the scope of this book. A major problem, for example, is how to best allocate multiple tasks between the individual processors without spending excessive amounts of time switching data and instructions back and forth between them. This is similar to the "thrashing" problem encountered when performing time-shared operations in large mainframe computers. With an inefficient operating system more time may be spent switching programs in and out of the main memory than is spent in the processing itself.

The third type of distributed processing was described in the earlier example of an application to the control of industrial plants. There are many similarities to the distributed EDP case; both consist of processors that are geographically dispersed, for example. The major difference is that the process control system employs its dispersed processors for independent tasks, and each is capable of performing its programs without the input of other processors, either on the same or higher level. It might be said that the industrial application is a case of "democratic" or peer cooperation between processors that are on the same level, while the EDP application is strictly hierarchal. In the EDP case the satellite processors and terminals, although they may perform a certain amount of local preprocessing, function largely to feed data into the CPUs. The industrial control type of distributed processing is, on the other hand, a truly parallel operation. It differs from the second kind of multiple processor (described above) by being "loosely coupled."

Communication links between processors are used primarily to bring summary data of the state of the controlled processes into a central area where they can be monitored and supervised by human operators. The communication links between peer processors are usually of a much lower order, being confined to emergencies (e.g., the replacement of failed units by standbys) or to situations where the process itself is interactive or "tightly coupled." The communication with operators must be bilateral, since they must have the option of altering the programmed goals of the distributed controllers, altering their interrelationships, or even of taking over direct control by specifying outputs, in the event that the process state differs from that desired.

HIERARCHAL PROCESSING LAYERS

The peer operation of the process (or machine) controllers and of those processors supporting the operator displays and controls does not exclude the possibility of a superimposed layer or layers of hierarchal computers above this peer group. For obvious reasons these are termed *supervisory computers.* They may supplement and to some extent replace the functions of the human operators and supervisors. But even in these cases the subordinate controllers and displays do not function as mere terminals, but continue to perform a significant real-time processing activity on their level. A good description of hierarchal control applied to a modern steel mill, given by Kahne, Lefkowitz, and Rose in *Scientific American,*[4] is pictured in Figure 7-2.

Of course it is entirely possible for supervisory computers to take over the entire control function, not only that of optimization, but the

A- Level Computers	1- Tape Of Product Orders
	2- Computers For Orders Processing, Material Requests, Production Scheduling
B- Level Computers	3- File Storage For Work Instructions, Production Status
	4- Daily Work Scheduling
C- Level Computers	5- On-Line Computer System For Work Instructions, Data Gathering
D- Level Computers	6- Input/Output Terminal And Operator Display Panel
	7- On-Line Process Control Computer
	8- Mini/Microcomputer For Direct Positioning And Sequencing Control Functions

Figure 7–2   Hierarchal levels of computer control in a modern steel mill. (Adapted from Kahne, Lefkowitz, and Rose.[4])

first level control of process valves and actuators. However, this function is usually not termed *supervisory* but rather *direct digital control* (DDC). Where it is necessary to coordinate the control of many interacting points in a system (such as the flow, level of fluids, and temperature or pressure of a fractionating column in a refinery), DDC is an acceptable alternative to increased communication between peer processors. If both modes are used in the same system, the subordinate processors may act merely as I/O devices, and so are analogous to the terminals (intelligent or otherwise) of the EDP system. However, we do not consider these cases to be distributed processing because the work is being done in a central machine.

COMMUNICATION SYSTEMS

This chapter is mainly concerned with distributed processors and communication between them in examples of this third kind. For satisfactory operation of the system at its highest level (with the supervision of humans or computers), the communication subsystem is vitally important. In most cases these systems are geographically confined to a moderate-sized area—say a few square miles. The communications systems are generally *dedicated,* that is, they do not use public facilities such as the telephone system. This is necessary for reasons of reliability, security, and availability. This type of communication system is also termed a *local network* and, because of the proliferation of industrial systems of the kind we have discussed, is of much current interest. Local networks are also being introduced into the office environment to link such devices as copiers and word processors. One such system is Ethernet,™ which is supported by the Xerox, Intel, and Digital Equipment Corporations.[5] In contrast, the EDP-type distributed systems normally use public communication such as telephones to link, for example, bank branches to a central processing facility.

The two types of communication systems, public and dedicated, have very different characteristics. The private network is in general much more secure; that is, it is less noisy and less subject to transient conditions such as those caused by switching. The private network can also be designed to operate at much higher speeds; for example, Ethernet operates at 10 megabits per second (Mbps) whereas the switched telephone network has an effective bandwidth of about 2500 hertz or less, and normally supports data transmission at speeds of up to 2400 bits per second (except when special-coded modems are used). Of course, the telephone system is already in place; it permits global communication and is available at a nominal rent. Even though it was not designed to carry digital data, the telephone system manages to handle a great deal of this kind of traffic without many problems. The private network, on the other hand, may be more effective but is often quite costly to install. (Since installation costs are proportional to cable feet, this is a reason why high speed serial cables such as coaxial cable are preferred to multiple dedicated signal pairs. This kind of local network is often called a *data highway.*)

ARCHITECTURE AND PROTOCOLS OF NETWORKS

The best of all possible worlds would be a combination of the privacy and security of the local network with the global connections of the public net. Such an architecture is called an *open system,* because any local network could be put into communication with any other net, given that both were open. We therefore discuss in this chapter the means by which a local network may be operated so as to reliably interconnect distributed processors and at the same time interface with the global public networks, that is, function as an open system. Note that it is not sufficient merely to tie together two systems physically. There are many levels of signals, symbols, and intelligence that must be matched before two systems can be made to communicate. The layers of meaning that must be coordinated are called the *protocol,* a term that we have briefly mentioned in an earlier chapter in conjunction with computer buses. We therefore undertake to explain the communication process between processors in terms of signals and protocols as well as architecture.

DIGITAL SIGNAL WAVEFORMS

At the most basic level of binary digital communication it is necessary to define a bit; what is to be called a "ONE" (historically, a "MARK" because of the marks made by the earliest recording telegraph instruments) and what is a "ZERO" (or "SPACE"). In the first chapter we defined the levels used by TTL electronics. Any signal level above 4.5 volts was defined as "1," and any level below 1.0 volt was defined as "0" in the logical sense. Another name for this scheme is *positive logic,* because the 1 is a high or assured positive voltage. We could also have defined the 1's and 0's oppositely, in which case we would call it *negative logic.* The agreement on the meaning of these signal levels and polarities enables the various parts of the processor and its peripherals to understand the data on the control and data buses and so act in a mutually consistent manner with respect to each other's signals.

This is an elementary form of protocol that is built into the hardware elements themselves. Since these are permanently wired together, there is no danger of misunderstanding, except in the cases of low signal to noise ratio or the timing problems arising in long parallel-signal buses, as discussed in earlier chapters. But when we leave the local domain of one processor and its immediate peripherals and venture into the larger world of distributed processing, there are many means of signals possible and many means of communicating bits that are chosen for a variety of reasons.

The first design decision that must be made is that of the physical connection or *link*. If the link is to be a continuous physical conductor such as a wire pair of a coaxial cable, a pulse of current can be used for the signal. Teletypes (TTY 20-milliampere current loops) are connected in this manner. If the line polarity or current is directly controlled by the logic level of the bits, the term used for this kind of communication is *baseband signaling.* A fiber optics line can also operate in the baseband mode. If on the other hand the logical signals modulate some type of carrier wave so that the logic levels are transformer connected to an audio or radio link, for example, we require a conversion device termed a *modem.* ("Modem" is simply an abbreviation for "modulator-demodulator.") Baseband signals require a band of frequencies ranging from about 0 hertz (DC) to a frequency approximately the same as the symbol rate. Modulated signals occupy higher frequencies and can also be "frequency modulated"; that is, several channels can be centered at different frequencies within a band traveling in the same medium. (This technique, however, is seldom used within local networks.)

Since baseband signals are the fundamental form, let us look at some of the possible arrangements and their relative advantages. Figure 7-3 shows a waveform in which the presence of current (ON) represents a mark of 1 and the absence of sensed current (OFF) is a space or 0. It is necessary to sample the waveform at known instants of time, which in turn are synchronized with the periods in which the steady state values of the symbols are achieved. In other words the transient waveform of the transmitter must be such as to guarantee that the current is above the threshold value at the sampling instant if the signal is to be recognized as a 1. Conversely, it must be guaranteed that the current value is less than the threshold at that instant if the symbol to be transmitted is a 0. This mechanism is therefore called a *synchronous ON-OFF signal*. Since there is no separation between two like symbols that are adjacent, such as the two 1's in the figure, this waveform is also known as a *nonreturn-to-zero* (NRZ) signal.

It is also possible to distinguish between mark and space by inverting the polarity of the current. The waveform would be identical to that of Figure 7-3 except that the "no-current" label would be "negative current," and the threshold of decision would be zero current rather than some positive value. The nonpolar waveform was used in historic telegraph instruments where the "sounders" were insensitive to the current direction. The polar signal has the advantage that a dead line (0 current) is not mistaken for a space.

Figure 7-4 takes this concept one step further by requiring a *return-to-zero* (RZ) signal between each mark or space. Thus either symbol is always heralded by a transition from zero. These transitions can be used as markers to measure the sampling instant, which should occur just after the new symbol wave reaches a steady value above or below its threshold. Now, since no synchronism is required between the

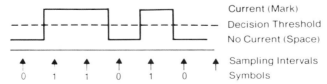

Figure 7–3 Synchronous ON-OFF waveforms for digital (binary) signaling (NRZ).

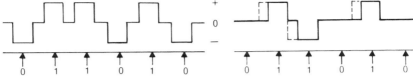

Figure 7–4   Polar return-to-zero, self-clocking digital signals.

Figure 7–5   Bipolar digital signal waveforms.

transmitter and receiver, the waveform is self-clocking, and the symbols can be sent at any irregular interval—they are *asynchronous*. Figure 7-4 shows a polar waveform, but the current could also be unidirectional as in Figure 7-3.

A useful variant of the polar signal is shown in Figure 7-5. Here the 1's are symbolized by transitions of alternate polarity and the 0's by no transition. This waveform is called *bipolar.* The effect of alternating the pulse polarity is to effectively eliminate direct current in the line. In the ordinary kind of polar waveform (Figure 7-4) there is a DC component due to the imbalance of 1's and 0's.

The bipolar signal also imposes a lower requirement on the high frequency end of the bandwidth than does the standard RZ form. This can be seen intuitively by comparing Figures 7-4 and 7-5. This fact is used in some types of digital facsimile transmitters to improve speed and resolution within the limited bandwidth of the telephone system.

All these waveforms employ only two amplitude levels to represent the two symbols 1 and 0. But most media, including the telephone network, are essentially analog and are capable of separating reliably many more levels of amplitude, as we observe when we transmit voice waveforms in these links. It would seem natural to take advantage of this capability and use several amplitude levels to represent groups of bits rather than a single 1 or 0. In this way, the characteristics of the medium can be utilized more efficiently and a significant saving in bandwidth can be achieved.

One way that this can be done is demonstrated in Figure 7-6, which shows the method of using multilevel signals.[6] In this example there are four amplitude levels that are significant and therefore three decision thresholds. Each level represents a pair of bits. In a practical device the bit stream to be transmitted would be assembled into pairs, and each pair (perhaps its binary numerical value, as shown) used to amplitude modulate the baseband waveform. This technique is also used in facsimile machines, where it is desired to operate at the highest speed within the limited bandwidth of the switched telephone network. Some

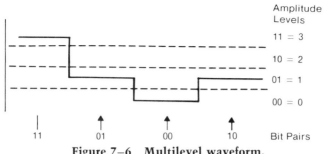

Figure 7-6 Multilevel waveform.

high speed machines use up to eight levels of amplitude. It can be seen that the saving in bandwidth is directly proportional to the number of levels of amplitude employed. Figure 7-6 represents approximately one cycle of bandwidth and carries 8 bits. A binary signal such as that shown in Figure 7-4 can carry at best 2 bits per cycle. The four-level waveform shown is synchronous, not self-clocking, but it is possible to extract synchronizing signals from the original binary wave.

One signal waveform that is widely used in modern transmission links for local networks is the Manchester or biphase code. This code is particularly suited for fiber optics transmission lines.[7] The Manchester inverts the phase of a complete cycle by 180 degrees to distinguish between the two binary symbols. This is shown in Figure 7-7. This code is self-clocking in baseband form and also adds security to the transmission scheme by allowing a complete bit check; that is, no symbol is accepted as a 0 or 1 bit unless it represents a complete cycle of modulation in either phase. The Manchester code can be transmitted at a bit rate (f_m) equal to 1.75 times the corner (-3 decibles) frequency for sine waves (f_0).

Each of the above baseband waveforms can be used to modulate another type of wave that might be suited to the medium with which we want to work. For example, the baseband can turn on and off a carrier wave (100% modulation) which might be a radio, wave, or light beam in a fiber optics cable. Alternatively, the baseband can modulate the frequency of the carrier (FM), shift between two frequencies (frequency-shift keying or FSK), or modulate the phase of the carrier as in the Manchester code. The baseband can also modulate the duration or position (in time) or another pulsed waveform. Discussion of these types of modulation, of which there are many combinations, are found in texts on communication and on telemetry in particular (e.g., see Ref. 6), and thus are not necessary here. However, it is interesting to look at one

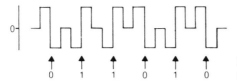

Figure 7–7 Manchester or phase modulation code.

kind of modulation that is commonly employed in microprocessor systems, that used by many systems of digital recording using magnetic tape cassettes.

Figure 7-8 shows the coding used by the Synertek SYM-1 microprocessor system for magnetic tape recording. A 0 is represented by a half-cycle of a 700-hertz waveform and a 1 by a full cycle of a 1400-hertz wave. The two symbols can be distinguished by the difference in adjacent zero-crossing time intervals of the composite alternating-current wave. A zero crossing at 450 microseconds (typically between 255 and 450) is interpreted as a 1 and anything over 450 is labeled an 0. Thus this waveform is similar to FSK modulation but, since it is not self-clocking, the bit stream must first be synchronized with the computer (receiver) by the transmission of a series of synch characters (16 hexadecimal in the SYM-1).

ARCHITECTURE OF LOCAL COMMUNICATION SUBSYSTEMS

A question that has been raised many times is whether there is a rationale to select a local communication architecture for a distributed computer system. It is apparent that there is not a clear or simple criterion or the question would not persist. The central problem may be stated as follows: Given a set of rules or protocol (of which more later) that determine which processor may use the communication link at any time, how shall this control be exerted? (For example, by central controller or "bus master" or by each processor in turn?) How shall we resolve *contention*, that is, where two or more processors wish to

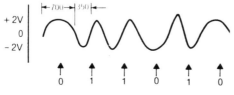

Figure 7–8 High-speed digital tape-recording format (FSK). (Adapted from SYM–1 Reference Manual.[8])

control the link at the same time? How can we establish reliability, that is, how to insure communication between undamaged processors in case one or more processors fail?

Part of the problem is that of nomenclature. There appears to be a lack of clear definition and agreement on what constitutes a particular architecture such as a "ring." We try to define these terms here. Because others may use a somewhat different interpretation, any taxonomy may be subject to challenge. Therefore it is a good idea to agree on exact terms before debating the merits of a particular structure.

Another part of the problem is its scope. Topology, which is the study of invariant properties of geometric shapes or connected networks (e.g., a continuous loop or ring has no ends regardless of how it is distorted), is clearly an important factor.[9] But architecture cannot be considered on the basis of topology alone, desirable as that may be. At least three elements must be considered: topology, or how the entities are connected; routing control, the rules by which entities are allowed to communicate (including protocol at the lower levels); and technology. Given these three factors, the decision elements of cost, reliability, complexity, distance, and so forth are subject to trade-offs. That is, some architectures may be inherently more resistant to some modes of failure than others, but all can be brought up to "satisfactory" levels by adding complexity (e.g., redundancy) at added cost. To attempt to bring the question down to manageable size, we address primarily the first two (topology and control). Since technology may be considered something of a common denominator, the improvement in bandwidth by using fiber optics, for example, is as beneficial to a ring as it is to a bus.

TOPOLOGY

Consider first a formless collection of entities, defined as those addressable elements that wish to communicate. We borrow the word *entity* rather than *unit* or *box*, because one possible mode of communication that might prove valuable is to address a software function or activity that may move from processor to processor. This would include, for example, the dynamic reallocation of a controller function, where we may not know in advance what box is performing the function. However, the function could be addressed and would respond from its present location. The word entity includes this possibility.

The first question to ask is how shall we control use of the medium? Will each entity be allowed to speak to any other (at the same time) or shall we exercise control over allocation of the medium? There is only one way that multiple entities can communicate simultaneously without garble, and that is by providing separate channels for each pair. Such a configuration is called a *mesh* or an *unconstrained* topology (Figure 7-9). This is obviously very expensive, so it is only used where the channels already exist and some benefit is obtained by providing the complex interconnection switches. The benefit of a mesh is the ability to support many simultaneous conversations or interconnections and find an optimum or a satisfactory path for each. While this is necessary for a telephone network or for a multiple-goal computing network (e.g., a time-share system), it is not obvious that this capability is needed in other applications such as a local process control function.

We can therefore consider only those that support a single speaker at any one time; that is, they are *constrained*. The constrained topologies can be considered as basically three—the star, ring, and bus. (The dropline bus is a variation of the bus that we also consider.) Figure 7-10 shows these topologies.

ROUTING CONTROL

The star network concentrates the control of communication in one central node. There is no decision to be made about who talks—only the central node can say. Therefore there is no direct communication between secondary nodes. The lack of decision required means that the mechanism of routing can be simple and reliable.

The star is an obvious choice if the communication pattern is primarily central-to-secondary nodes. This would be the case in a central computer control system or with a computer time-sharing with dumb terminals, such as a bank EDP system with remote terminals for automatic tellers.

When the normal communication pattern is between secondary nodes, the star is less favorable. Communication is slowed, the central node is a bottleneck, or it must devote too much of its expensive

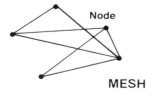

MESH

Figure 7–9   Mesh (unconstrained) network topology.

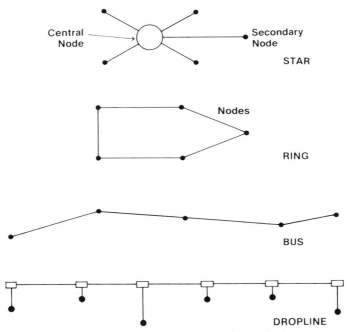

Figure 7–10   Constrained network topologies.

resources to servicing its satellite's communication needs. Some of the load on the central (host) processor can be relieved by using a communication front end processor, but this again adds complexity and cost to the system. The reliability of the network depends fully on the central node. Therefore the cost and effort of making it reliable enough may be more than the saving in simplifying the routing control of the secondaries.

The ring eliminates the central node as a controller, but requires some additional elements in all its nodes. The ring function requires that each node send its message to the next node in the ring, unidirectionally. Thus the control rule is very simple. The message goes around the ring from node to node until it is found by the intended receiver. If the receiver then removes the message from the network (thus conserving operating time), the ring is operating in a *point-to-point* mode. If the message continues around the ring until it comes back to the originator, the ring is acting in a *broadcast* mode. This would be used in polling, for example, where there is no address or to look for a process (entity) for which the address is not known but is recognized by the node in which it resides.

The bus structure is similar to the ring in that there is no central control. In the pure bus any node that originates a message sends it in both directions until it reaches the end. The intended node must also be able to recognize and read the message as it goes by. The bus structure thus acts in a broadcast mode. The dropline bus variant is similar to the pure bus except that all dropline interface units hear the message simultaneously (neglecting line delays), so there is no pass–along.

We thus have two major factors, topology and control. The topology may be star, ring, or bus; the control, central or distributed. Any combination can be used. Figure 7-11 shows a taxonomical arrangement of feasible combinations.

For example, a ring can be centrally controlled (a Bell Labs system, SPIDER, to do this has been described). The protocol SDLC can be used to centrally control ring or multidrop bus topologies. A ring topology has been used with contention control, which is described in the next section.

CONTROL STRUCTURES

The control structure in a distributed network determines what node transmits at any particular time. This is only a problem for ring and bus topologies.

One mechanism is the *daisy chain*, which is used in ring structures to pass permission to use the bus from one node to the next. It consists of dedicated wires, or *grant lines*. Since these must be connected between each pair, they involve unwanted installation expense.

Another mechanism is the *control token*. This is a small bit pattern, for example, 8 bits, that is passed from node to node. Any node, on receiving the token, can remove it from the ring, insert a message, and then pass on the token. The token eliminates the dedicated wires, but precautions must be taken to prevent a decrease in reliability. Since the token is small, not much overhead is used.

Alternatively, the ring can circulate message *slots* that are big enough to hold an entire message. Any slot marked "empty" can be filled with a message and passed on. Several slots can be circulated at one time, as distinguished from the single token. However, the greater size of the slot compared to the token may result in more overhead if the slots are empty. The slot technique is not fully distributed, since one node must generate slots. Another technique involves register insertion; a shift register is loaded with a message and then inserted in the net at an idle time. It must then be shifted out again for reuse. This method

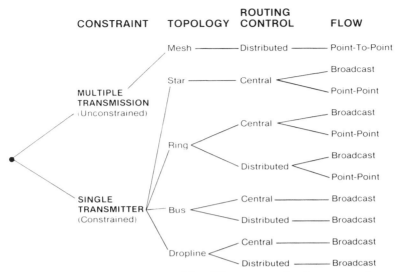

Figure 7–11   Taxonomy of feasible communication networks.

is somewhat complex and subject to problems if the message is "damaged"; distorted before being shifted out.

The above structures are appropriate for rings. A good control structure for a bus is contention; that is, any node wishing to transmit merely does so. If two try simultaneously, the messages are garbled in what is called a *collision*. The lost messages must then be transmitted after a random wait. This requires much bandwidth (overhead), but actually it has been shown that only about 1/2e or 18.4% maximum of the bandwidth can be used to carry new messages (*throughput*).[10] The remainder are retransmitted messages. But a big advantage of contention is simplicity and reliability. If a control token or any other ring control mechanism is destroyed by a transient, the ring must be able to start itself again. But with a decentralized system there is a question of how to detect failure and what node has the right to restart. Although in contention there is no control entity to be destroyed, we need some higher level protocol to say whether a message has been garbled to be able to detect a collision.

The original radio broadcast contention system (developed at the University of Hawaii) is called *Aloha*. The Ethernet cabled system mentioned earlier is also a contention system. There are a variety of Alohas combining contention with slots (slotted Aloha), in which each user can start (re) transmission only at the beginning of a time period equal to message length. Another variant of Aloha (CSMA, developed at Stanford University) requires the sender to listen before transmitting. These methods can improve the theoretical throughput (fraction of new messages) up to 80%.

RELIABILITY CONSIDERATIONS

The objective of ring and bus structures is to eliminate the unreliable feature of the star, central control. Whenever we do not have a completely distributed structure, we are vulnerable in that regard. Of course we are speaking only of the inherent reliability of the design—added protection is gained by redundancy and more expensive technology.

Of the ring and the bus topologies, both fully distributed, the conventional ring is the more vulnerable because of the need for an active repeater at each node (to remove the message or pass it on). Also, the control strategy, such as token removal, must be implemented. Failure of any part of this logic can destroy the function of the network. Thus repeaters have to be very reliable.

It is not always true that a ring will keep functioning if a node fails. Provisions must be made to remove the node from the ring to localize the failure.

The bus does not require active repeaters at each node. Each node can be a passive listener. Therefore the node can fail without disrupting the bus as long as it presents a high impedance to the line.

There is one flaw to this bus advantage. If the transmission line is struck by lightning, for example, only those elements connected to the line would be expected to be destroyed. In the case of the ring this would be one set of receivers and one set of line drivers. In the case of the bus it would be all nodes. Thus while both would be damaged, it would take longer to repair the bus.

SUMMARY OF ARCHITECTURE

It would be simplistic to conclude on the basis of these considerations alone that a bus with contention control or some other configuration is the most desirable. Too much is dependent on factors such as traffic patterns, environment, and technology. Therefore we are forced to conclude that there is no simple answer to the question of what is the "best" architecture. At least one other factor that must be considered is protocol.

PROTOCOL

In a communication channel shared by many users, protocol is the totality of rules and structure that determine how each entity must interact with others to accomplish the objectives of the community. In a homely example small children at the dinner table should not interrupt their parents' conversation (except in an emergency such as spilling their milk). Thus protocol includes such things as identification of speaker and listener, brevity of message, confirmation, repetition, and coding.

Symbol coding, as described earlier, is included in protocol but is not the only factor involved in protocol.

Protocol exists, or should exist, because it is necessary to accomplish our purpose in a certain environment. This environment includes the architecture of the network and the message structure (broadcast, point-to-point, virtual circuit), the bandwidth or message rate required, the delays that can be tolerated, error rate, line speed, propagation delay (distance), error and loss control means, noise in the line, use of common carrier or all-dedicated lines, and so on. This means that protocol design can be a very complicated subject, and is by no means independent of the hardware and software of the processors utilizing the communication link. In fact, there can be much trade-off with software complexity.

Protocol can be considered to consist of layers. A *layer* is an entity that can be used by any higher process (layer) without regard to its internal structure; that is, successively higher layers are independent.[13] The technique of protocol layering is thus similar to that discussed under structured programming. For example, at the bottom layer is the basic function of delivering a package of bits to a specific entity and assuring that the package is not damaged. The meaning of the data bits is not known at this level. The next layer considers groups of words or packets as messages. This is accomplished by interpretation of a "Word ID" field, which tells us to look for data or a control signal or whatever. A layer that is higher yet might be a fairly lengthy and complicated interchange of information between two or more processors. We can envision even higher layers to solve particular problems of communication, such as error recovery or downloading of files or programs. The International Standards Organization (ISO) has promulgated a seven-layer protocol standard that we review further on.[11,12]

Protocol design is by no means a science yet, but is in a state analogous to the early days of computer software, when there was first ad hoc machine coding, then rudimentary languages, then HLLs such as BASIC and FORTRAN, which use subroutines. Now we are using structured programming where programs are modular and interconnected, grammar, and theories and proofs of correctness. We are approaching the time when much programming will be mechanized. Protocol development is also going through these stages, and now *protocol languages* are being developed.[13] Pascal, for example, is well structured for protocol design. These are being implemented in such programs as ARPAnet, the DOD's system of nationwide interconnected computers. Protocol development is in a dynamic state. Furthermore, the few large distributed systems such as ARPAnet on which most research effort has been expended are so complex that all the answers are not yet in on their protocol designs (see Ref. 10).

DATA LINK PROTOCOLS

The level of protocol of most immediate concern to the microprocessor system designer is that of the data link. This includes the function of framing, identification of transmitter and intended recipient, line control, error control, synchronization, and other features concerned with transport of a message from the transmitting end of a link to the receiver. Any line control must enable the connection between the two ends to be established, initiate synchronism to allow bits to be recognized and a message sent, and terminate the correction when completed so that the line is free for other users. Framing constitutes the rules that establish which bits are messages and which are synchronizing or control characters. Error control implies a means of checking on the accuracy of the transmission, usually by means of redundant bits (see Chapter 1). In the event that messages are broken up into standard-length packets without regard to their context and transmitted on arbitrary paths, some means must be provided to number and sequence them so that they be reconstructed in proper order.

Control codes are used as part of the data link protocol to signal such events as the start of text (SOT), acknowledgment of receipt (ACK), and similar functions. The ANSI Data Link Control (the US standard) uses 10 of the possible 128 seven-bit characters of the ASCII code for line control. For example, ACK is 000 0110, NACK (negative acknowledgement from the receiver) is 0010101, and the synchronous idle character SYN that begins all transmission in this protocol is 001 0110. The use of central characters introduces the problem of *transparency*, or how to transmit message text in which characters combine to give the same bit patterns as the control symbol.

The contents of the message frame can be interpreted as bits, bytes, or characters, and protocols can be established for any of these. The most general is the bit-oriented protocol, in which the message is transparent. The high level data link control (HDLC), derived by ISO, and the similar synchronous data link control (SDLC), introduced by IBM, are examples of bit-oriented protocols, but other new arrangements are being adopted by different organizations.

An explanation of the SDLC format gives the flavor of all these types of protocols and will enable the reader to understand others as they are introduced. To evaluate them, recall that the functions specified at the beginning of this section may be subject to the following applications: [14]

Conversational: short messages, fast response, with low overhead.
Inquiry-response: short input, long output.
Batch: large quantities of data.
Space satellite: large propagation delays; requires block numbering because of delay of ACK message.

Since many of these applications do not apply in specific situations, such as some local networks, protocols may be desired that are more specific and more efficient in their limited application. This explains the proliferation of "standards" that do not conform to the "open network" principle established earlier as a desired goal.

Figure 7-12 shows that the HDLC (and SDLC) frames are enclosed between two *flags*, identical bit patterns that serve to establish bit synchronization and signify the beginning and end of the frame. The unique pattern is

$$01111110$$

The flags must be unique patterns to ensure transparency because the length of the frame is not fixed. The information "field" within the frame is of variable size. If a flag pattern were to appear inadvertently within the information field, for example, the frame would be prematurely terminated. To prevent this a technique called *bit stuffing* is used. Since the six 1-bit pattern of the flag is unique, wherever five

Figure 7–12   SDLC frame (HDLC is similar).

1-bits are encountered within the frame a 0 is inserted by special circuitry within the transmitter. The 0-bit insertion technique applies to all the fields (address, control, information, and block check) between the two flags.[15]

The field following the opening flag is an 8-bit station address, which can refer to any of 256 potential receivers or groups of receivers. In other protocols the address field may be expanded to include an identification of the transmitter as well as the receiver. Thus the address field(s) could be comprised of 16 bits or more.

The byte following the address field in SDLC is the control field. This indicates which mode of operation is being employed by this frame, the choices being I for information transfer, S for supervisory, and US (or U) for nonsequenced (unnumbered) frames. Only in the I mode is information (data) transferred. In the other two modes the control field bits are used to transmit or request the frame sequence count, indicate the final frame in a sequence, or as a polling means. (Note that some of these functions are really not a part of line protocol layer in the ISO sense, but should be reserved for a higher layer.)

The information frame is optional and may only be included in an I-mode control format. The length of this field in SDLC is unconstrained. In other frame protocols it may be an integral number of bytes. Owing to the bit-stuffing techniques, the information field may contain any bit sequence, and is only interpreted in a higher layer.

The field before the final flag is a block check, which is a code calculated by dividing the transmitted data bits (considered as a binary number) by a *generator* number (polynomial) and using the computed remainder. At the receiver end a similar calculation is made, and the two block checks compared. This is a very powerful means of detecting and/or correcting errors, and is used to control the ACK, NACK, and retransmission functions of the error control layer.

It can be seen that HDLC/SDLC and their derivations are a very flexible means of controlling the data link, and can function in all the environments specified earlier. They are obviously not efficient if only short messages are to be exchanged because of the high overhead implied by the framing and control. In communication parlance they utilize a great deal of link bandwidth. Nevertheless, the importance of open systems in today's multiprocessor links means that this type of protocol will be widely employed.

ETHERNET—A CONTENTION SYSTEM

The bit-oriented frame protocols such as HDLC/SDLC ensure safe delivery of data and recognition of errors to implement recovery procedures, but they do not solve the problem of multiple transmitters contending for control of the line. "Bus mastership" is considered to be the function of a higher protocol layer. SDLC, in fact, assumes that one station (called the *primary station*) has control of the line at all times. We have mentioned in the architecture discussion other means of allocating the link, including the use of a token as in a ring system. Another method now coming into use is *contention*. When this method is used, any station can transmit at any time, but if two attempt to do so simultaneously, they must "back off" and retransmit. If each station waits a random time before retransmitting, eventually one will find a clear spot. Of course, this requires recognition of a garbled transmission. By using some sort of link protocol such as HDLC, a frame garbled by multiple transmission will appear to be damaged by noise and will not elicit an ACK, thus triggering error-recovery retransmissions. As indicated earlier, methods such as listening to the carrier medium before transmitting improve the efficiency of the system. Ethernet uses such a *carrier sense mechanism* (CSMA), as distinguished from its Aloha forebear. Each sender monitors the carrier ("ether") during transmission and detects a collision when the signal does not match its own output.[16]

The Ethernet architecture consists of two layers, called the *physical layer* and the *data link layer*. These are intended to support the ISO seven-layer model. The higher layers include the network layer, which is responsible for routing and delivering the message; the transport layer, which handles end-to-end error and flow control; and the session, presentation, and application layers, which are concerned with the meaning of the messages rather than their mere delivery as packages of bits. All these are considered by Ethernet as the responsibility of the user, hence are lumped in the "client layer."

The goals of Ethernet are stated as

Simplicity.
Low cost.
Compatibility (with all other Ethernets).
Addressing flexibility (to any mode or group).
Fairness (equal access of all nodes averaged over time).
Progress (no blocking of other by any node).
High speed (10 megabits).
Low delay in frame transfer.
Maintainability.
Layered architecture as above.

Nongoals of Ethernet are

Full duplex—data are transferred in only one direction at a time. High speed enables bidirectional communication.

Error control—only recovery from collisions is provided; other errors are corrected by higher layers.

Security encryption (secure coding)—this is the responsibility of higher layers; if it is wanted.

Speed flexibility—the speed is fixed at 10 megabits per second.

Priority—all stations have equal priority in use at the bus.

Hostile user—there is no protection from this danger in the network.

DATA LINK LAYER

Ethernet is a broadcast network; that is, all stations use the same medium ("ether"). The data link layer is not identical to the physical connection, as it would be in a direct point-to-point connection. The main data link control functions are

1   Data encapsulation.

    Framing the message.

    Addressing—source and destination error detection.

2   Link management.

    Channel allocation (collision avoidance).

    Contention resolution (collision handling).

Some idea of the data link format can be obtained.

Preamble: 64 encoded bits (1010 . . .) are transmitted (by the physical layer) to allow synchronization of clocks before each frame.

Destination address: 6 octets (8 bits each) specify the station or stations for which the frame is intended.

Source address: 6 octets specify the sending station.

Type field: 2 octets are reserved for use by higher levels (client protocol).

Data field: 46 to 150 octets (bytes) of data can be in this field.

Frame check sequence: the frame check is a 4-octet (32-bit) cyclic redundancy check that consists of a binary arithmetic operation on the bits of the other fields, which operation is checked at the receiver to detect collision or other errors, similar to the SDLC block check.

PHYSICAL LAYER

The main element of the physical layer is a single 10 megabit per second coaxial cable channel. The functions of this layer are

Data encoding.
Preamble, for synchronization bit encoding and decoding.
Channel access.
Bit transmission and reception.
Carrier sense (sensing traffic on the channel).
Collision detection (contention sensing).

The preamble has already been explained. The bit encoding is phase (Manchester), which combines separate clock and data signals into a single serial bit stream. As explained earlier, the Manchester code transmits the logical complement of the bit value during the first half of a bit cell (a cell is 100 nanoseconds for a 10 megabit per second bus) and the uncomplemented value during the second half. Thus there is always a signal transition in either the positive or negative direction in the center of each bit cell.

The physical layer protocol specifies the characteristics necessary to ensure that all Ethernets are compatible. These include data encoding, timing, and voltage levels (±700 millivolts into 78 ohms). The details of how these are to be implemented are deliberately left unsaid. However, all Ethernets use standard coaxial cable up to 500 meters in length and can use inexpensive taps, such as those used by cable television for each station.

Ethernet is relatively new and is only one of several local area communication systems that have been developed for multiple computer networks. (Others include the Ungermann-Bass Net/One, the Zilog Inc. Z-Net, and those offered by Wang Laboratories Inc. and Datapoint Inc.)[17] Ultimately the acceptance of these systems will depend on their long-term record of performance and reliability. Shock and Hupp[16] have reported tests on one system spanning 1800 feet and connecting 120 machines. This network carries up to 300 million bytes per day and remains stable up to 97% of channel utilization. (This is an old system running at 2.94 megabits per second.)

The packet error rate is about one in 2 million (roughly one per day). The overall utilization of the bus is less than 1%, but instantaneously it can rise to 37% in 1 second. The traffic is bimodal and most packets are short (ACKS, etc.), but most volume is in large file transfer packets, up to 560 bytes.

Over 99% of the packets are sent out immediately; less than 1% are delayed because of collision or sensing a busy cable. The data fields transmitted represent about 79% of all bits overall; about 21% of the bits encompass all forms of overhead.

LOCAL DATA NETS FOR INDUSTRY

Ethernet and many of its contemporaries are intended for use in the "automated office." In transmission of business data and graphical material such as facsimile, the loss of a single bit or packet may not be catastrophic. Furthermore, variation in delay in delivery of any one packet may not be extremely important as long as the network keeps up with the offered load.

In industrial situations, such as control of a plant or process, there is quite a different situation. Reliability of transmission of control signals is of the utmost importance. The undetected distortion of a single bit could lead to a dangerous situation, such as sensing a switch OFF when it was actually ON. Of course, the application layers of protocol do everything possible to check errors in important parameters. Delay in message transmission, if measured in milliseconds, may not be crucial or even of much importance, so long as it is a *known* and *predictable* delay. (In a closed loop control system it is possible to compensate for fixed time lags, known as *transport delay*, if they are predictable, but if not they can lead to instability and cycling of the process. (See Ref. 2 for a fuller explanation of this phenomenon.)

The above consideration would lead one to believe that a network protocol more predictable than the CSMA-CD (contention) system is preferred for process and machine control situations. Of course there may be many situations in which these criteria would not apply, but in general industrial users would prefer a system that is more positive and predictable, such as a ring with token passing. For example, although the exact analysis of a ring rotating a token among multiple queues of messages is mathematically difficult, it is relatively easy to compute the maximum time to receive the token for a useful protocol (e.g., one that limits the time of bus use for any one station).

PROWAY

Because of the special requirements of local area networks in plant control situations it is not surprising that solutions proposed for these applications differ from Ethernet and others oriented toward data communications. One such program is the Proway project (Proway: a process data highway), which was begun by the International Electrotechnical Commission meeting in Moscow in 1975 and is now proceeding through the specification stage.[18,19]

One stated objective of Proway is to permit interconnection of process control systems and computers produced by different manufacturers, although the compatibility of signals alone (ISO data link layer) does not guarantee compatibility in the application or higher layers. Another objective is to minimize the chance of error. Since process control signals involve the movement of energy and materials, errors are of far greater significance for potential costly damage than signals that merely represent data records. The Proway goal for data integrity is one error per 1000 years (compare with the previously cited results of one error per day with an Ethernet).

ORGANIZATION OF PROWAY

Proway stations are organized into six ranks or types. As many as 100 stations may be located on a highway, although a much smaller number (about 30) is typical. The ranks, which represent highway functions, are

Manager (highest rank).
Supervisor.
Demander.
Initiator.
Responder.
Listener (lowest rank).

Each station must have at least one of these functions. It is designated by the highest function it performs.

Functions common to all ranks include

1   Maintaining the time sequence of all frames at the destination in the same order as seat (i.e., the order of control commands must not be inverted).

2   Supporting extended addressing and control structures.
3   Notifying the next higher rank of any errors that it cannot correct.

In addition, each rank has specialized functions as follows:

Listener: accepts all correct frames of interest to its station.
Responder: not only accepts frames addressed to it, but immediately acknowledges the frame and responds as appropriate.
Initiator:

1   responds to a supervisor's poll with a request for access to the highway.
2   transmits frames to listeners.
3   selects a responder by transmitting its address.
4   detects failure of responder to accept frame and initiates recovery procedures.

Demander: Transmits an unsolicited request through the data highway, usually a mode used by a candidate initiator. The request for initiator status may be by dedicated lines or special signals or states.
Supervisor: Performs the following tasks:

1   Controls line access (selects active initiators).
2   Arbitrates contention among active demanders or candidate initiators.
3   Monitors initiator activity and deals with errors.
4   Limits transaction time and traffic to keep any initiator from overloading the highway.
5   Insures continuity of highway operation if an active initiator fails.
6   Monitors performance of data path (integrity). Activates alternate data paths when there are unrecoverable errors or when the line is cut or disturbed.
7   Other functions such as transmitting global frames (those addressed to all stations).

Manager function: The manager monitors performance of all stations, assigns the active supervisor and resolves contention, and ensures continuity of data highway operation if the active supervisor fails.

TIMING AND APPLICATION

The timing of a process control function is critical, since lags in a control function can lead to counterproductive instability in the controlled process, for example, 180-degree phase lag (see Ref. 2). In Proway a typical application meets the following requirements of timing:

1   Access time of active demander less than 2 milliseconds if the frame transmission time is not over 1.5 milliseconds.
2   Access time of candidate initiator less than 20 milliseconds if the frame transmission time is not over 5 milliseconds.
3   Access time of candidate supervisor typically less than 1 second.

Any process control data highway must adapt to a broad range of applications having high or low information transfer rates. The highway and station may be located entirely within a protected control room (usually air-conditioned) or in the plant environment exposed to industrial hazards and electrical noise. It may be in a geographically small plant or spread over a large area such as a tank farm.

A local area Proway data highway in a control room may typically have a transmission line length of 200 meters and a high information rate of 100,000 bits per second, or one that traverses a large plant may have a length of 2000 meters and a lower information rate of 30,000 bits per second. Substantially higher requirements may be demanded by more sophisticated applications and systems.

In general, process control data highways such as Proway are characterized by event-driven communication, enabling them to respond to events as they happen (as opposed to waiting for polls), very high availability and data integrity, proper operation in the presence of electrical interference and imbalanced grounds, and the use of dedicated transmission lines. A special demand of Proway is that it be able to support direct data interchange between any two stations without involving a "store-and-forward" at a third station.

PROTOCOLS

Proway, like Ethernet, is designed as layers of protocol. The protocol functions in each layer must do the following:

1   Transfer data with high integrity, check for errors, and use recovery procedures.

2   Notify the next higher layer if it cannot correct errors.

3   Support communication of any arbitrary data in the information field of the frame passed to it from a higher layer.

4   Be completely logical and predictable in every conceivable transaction sequence and exit to an acceptable state.

5   Be transparent to transmission line lengths and data signaling rates (except for line couplers).

6   Allow the number of stations connected to highway to be changed.

7   Allow the mode and status of stations to be changed.

8   Support the monitoring and recording of communication performance.

In addition the line coupler protocol must convert frames from their internal (software) representation in the station to a form acceptable to the transmission line. These functions include converting signal levels or formats, providing galvanic (electrically conductive) isolation, generating and detecting frame synchronization and monitor signal quality, adding and removing frame delimiters (preambles, postambles), detecting transmission line states (busy or idle), and synchronizing initiators, responders, and listeners.

The frame structure for Proway is a variant of the HPLC previously described. A source address must be added to transfer the active initiator attribute and to permit a guaranteed access time, a Proway objective.

Note also that the information field in a highway frame may vary widely in length, typically from 2 to 1024 bytes.

Electrically, the RS-449 signal has been suggested as a Proway standard. The RS-449 is a successor to the RS-232, and consists of a 2-megabaud 37-conductor line not exceeding 50 feet in length.

INTEGRITY AND AVAILABILITY

The requirement of one error per 1000 years depends on the circuit bit error rate being less than one in a million and a frame length of less than 100 bits. An error-correction code including the complete frame (exclusive of synchronizing signals) must reduce the residual (undetected) error rate to 3×10^{-15}.

The data highway must operate in an electrically noisy environment without losing bits or frame sequence. This noise may range from 10 volts peak to peak at 400 hertz or less within a control room environment to 50 volts in a plant environment.

In general, no single communication failure should cause failure of the entire control system or any of its functions. This means that sufficient redundancy must be provided to distribute essential functions. In simplest terms this means that bus mastery shall be distributed. In addition, it means that the system will tolerate a change in configuration (station functions) while continuing to operate.

NETWORKING IN GENERAL

Ethernet and Proway are two examples of special kinds of communication networks that operate between computers and microprocessors and that were designed for special purposes. It is to be hoped that they are optimized for the environment of the automated office and the factory or process plant. There are, of course, much wider forms of digital networks, such as the AT&T Dataphone Service and ARPAnet. These are used for commercial and research information transfer and for ordinary communication between individuals, but mostly for corporate business purposes, such as funds transfer. In the last few years, however, a completely new form of network has sprung up, one that is based on personal microcomputers. Typical of these are The Source and MicroNET, which give owners of small computers access to games, business programs, storage, and other subscribers.[20] It is not even necessary to have a computer to access these networks; a dumb terminal and a modem will suffice. Other forms of networks are strictly amalgamations of standalone personal computers. The advantage here is to multiply the power of the individual computer by sharing expensive peripherals such as disk storage. It has been shown, for example, that a local network of 20 stations such as Apple II computers gives each user twice the computer power for half the cost of a time-shared minicomputer.[21]

The significance of these developments in computer communication is that for the first time in history significant computing and telecommunication power has been placed in the hands of individuals, rather than corporations or government agencies. According to authorities such as J. C. R. Licklider,[22] this power, if properly channeled by government and wisely used, has the ability to transform our lives profoundly. An immense data base and the capabilities to manipulate it would be in the hands of the ordinary citizen, even those who are now computer illiterates. The more powerful microprocessors (termed *mainframes on a chip*) now becoming available will be capable of utilizing the results of artificial intelligence research, programs that are "friendly" and adaptable to human imprecision, and will even accept speech rather than keyboard input. In such a knowledge-based society use of these powerful machines linked by a universal network can result in rapid improvements in every aspect of everyday life, such as shopping, working, medical care, security, assistance to the handicapped, and education. The advent of microprocessors brought into reality the concept of automation, the "second industrial revolution." The addition of networking to the proliferation of microcomputers will bring on a third wave, "computer power to the people." As Licklider states, "The information revolution is bringing with it a key that may open the door to a new era of involvement and participation. The key is the self-motivating exhilaration that accompanies truly effective interaction with information and knowledge through a . . . good network." Those of you who are helping to facilitate the marriage of microprocessors and communications systems may feel assured that you are making a contribution to world progress.

REFERENCES

1. *KTM-2 and KTM-2/80 Reference Manual*, Santa Clara, Calif.: Synertek Systems Corp. (1979).

2. Bibbero, R. J., *Microprocessors in Instruments and Control*, New York: Wiley-Interscience (1977), Chapter 9.

3. Davis, G. B. *Management Information Systems*, New York: McGraw-Hill (1974), pp. 248–252.

4. Kahne, S. et al., "Automatic Control by Distributed Intelligence," *Scientific American*, 78–90 (June 1979).

5. *The Ethernet: A Local Area Network*, Version 1.0, Palo Alto, Calif.: Xerox Corp.

6. Bennett, W. R., and Davey, J. R., *Data Transmission*, New York: McGraw-Hill (1965), p. 29.

7. Freeborn, J. C., *Electronic Design*, 3, 74–76 (February 1, 1979).

8. *SYM-1 Reference Manual*, Santa Clara, Calif.: Synertek Systems Corp. (June 1979), Appendix C.

9. Barr, S., *Experiments in Topology*, New York: Crowell (1964).

10. Kleinrock, L., *Proceedings of the IEEE*, **66**, 1327 (November 9, 1978).

11. International Organization for Standardization (ISO), "Reference Model of Open System Interconnection," *Document No. ISO/TC97/SC16 N227* (June 1979).

12. Zimmerman, H., "OSI Reference Model," *IEEE Transactions on Communication* (COM-28), 4 (April 1980).

13. Pouzin, L., and Zimmerman, H., "A Tutorial on Protocols," *Proceedings of the IEEE*, **66**, 1360 (November 1978).

14. Schwartz, M., *Computer-Communication Network Design and Analysis*, Englewood Cliffs, NJ: Prentice-Hall (1977), p. 335.

15. Donnan, R. A., and Kersey, J. R., *Synchronous Data Link Control: A Perspective*, TR29.0114, February 1974, IBM Systems Development Division, Research Triangle Park, N.C.

16. Sheck, J., and Hupp, J., "Performance of an Ethernet Local Network," Xerox Palo Alto Research Center, Palo Alto, Calif. (May 1979).

17. *Electronics*, 89–90 (June 5, 1980).

18. McGowan, U., "The Proway Project," *Control Engineering*, 29–34 (August 1979).

19. International Electro-technical Commission: Sub-Committee 65A, *Draft-Process Data Highway (Proway) for Distributed Control Systems* (March 1979).

20. Mazur, K., "Computer Networking," *Personal Computing*, 58–63 (September 1980).

21. Saal, H., Shustek, L., and Stretler, E., "Local Computer Networks of Personal Computers," paper at ACU Regional Conference on Distributed Processing, San Francisco (November 12–14, 1980).

22. Licklider, J. C. R., "Computers in Government," in *The Computer Age: A Twenty-Year View*, M. L. Dertougos and J. Moses (eds.), Cambridge, Mass.: MIT (1980), pp. 87–126.

Index